RESCUE WORK

RESCUE WORK

A Personal Reflection

ANDREW MICHAEL DOIG

Copyright © 2018 Andrew Michael Doig

The moral right of the author has been asserted.

Apart from any fair dealing for the purposes of research or private study, or criticism or review, as permitted under the Copyright, Designs and Patents Act 1988, this publication may only be reproduced, stored or transmitted, in any form or by any means, with the prior permission in writing of the publishers, or in the case of reprographic reproduction in accordance with the terms of licences issued by the Copyright Licensing Agency. Enquiries concerning reproduction outside those terms should be sent to the publishers.

Matador
9 Priory Business Park,
Wistow Road, Kibworth Beauchamp,
Leicestershire. LE8 0RX
Tel: 0116 279 2299
Email: books@troubador.co.uk
Web: www.troubador.co.uk/matador
Twitter: @matadorbooks

ISBN 978 1789013 962

British Library Cataloguing in Publication Data.
A catalogue record for this book is available from the British Library.

Printed and bound by CPI Group (UK) Ltd, Croydon, CR0 4YY
Typeset in 12pt Aldine401 BT by Troubador Publishing Ltd, Leicester, UK

Matador is an imprint of Troubador Publishing Ltd

This book is dedicated to all those who have generously tried to help humanity.

CONTENTS

Preface	ix
Willow Circle	1
Meetings With Doris	64
Closed Circle	84
Personal Opinion	128
The Astral World	141
Conclusions	144

Preface

Near the end of 2016, I typed out a record of the first closed circle that I had been part of until it closed in April 1996. Although my time there had only been less than 15 months (once a week except for holidays and illness etc.), it had been a formative experience at a time when I was at the start of my journey seeking the 'truth'. What many call 'Rescue Work' had been part of it, and indeed part of subsequent learning with Doris Lowe and another closed circle. I therefore decided to combine all these in one volume and then try to make an opinion on what it meant to me.

Doris Lowe gave others and myself teaching on many aspects of Spiritualism, roughly one day a month, from early 1997 to October 2000. This was at Kings Laggan, near Gatehouse of Fleet, in the south west of Scotland. She gave this free of charge, indeed, included was lunch as well as tea and biscuits, with many books and papers lent for those interested.

The final section is that which I experienced in a second closed circle, that ran from December 2006 until August 2011; again this sat once a week. The 'Rescue Work' here lasted only a few months, starting to occur about a year after the circle was formed. Only those aspects that touch on 'Rescue' or 'Saving lost Souls' are included after the Willow Circle.

Many people dislike these epithets, thinking them exaggerated and overblown, and I tend to agree. However, I will leave that to the final chapter, when I hope to explain my own personal opinions on the subject.

To those who may be new to this subject, I should explain exactly what a 'circle' is. It is where a number of people come together, for meditation, visualisation, healing, or to get in touch with those in spirit. This last point would be called a séance, a French word that originates from the Latin 'sedere' which means to 'sit'. People sit in a rough circle facing the centre; thereby all can see each other. There are 'open' circles that anybody can attend. However, all the circles mentioned in this book were 'closed', restricted to only certain people.

The only other point that I wish to explain is the ending of some sentences, when dialogue is recorded. When a person has paused, and another person has started conversation *after* that pause, the first person's sentence will end thus: ..." When the first person has been interrupted in their talking, their sentence will end thus: .."

Willow Circle

At the end of 1994, I was invited to join a private development group. This was the first such group that I had sat in, as all the others were either connected to spiritual healing or just meditation. What follows is an account of those meetings of this circle, those that I attended, taken from the notes that I made afterwards and some from tape recordings. The first meeting occurred on the 1st December, assembling in Bernard Kirby's house, with Mike and Audrey Peachey, Stan, Bernard, myself, but SA was absent. Mike gave an opening address and then we went into a meditation in silence. During this I saw a woman's face, which was framed by a hooded cloak, and the background was very dark with some light coloured 'twigs' standing out, as they seemed to have frost on them.

Shortly after this Audrey's breathing got louder and heavier and then her Chinaman (Chi) came through, very clearly and easily. He said that we were the right mix of energies and that another would be a channel (SA?). We did not yet have the energies at the right level, but that this would come. We could help this process by practicing more meditation, if only for a few minutes. We could open out our three highest chakras, like a flower unfolding, and project out the colours, at the same time bringing in the white and gold light into the centre, which would protect us. The group should meet regularly and ask (in time) to be put in touch with the 'higher entities'. He said that he was only on the medium level, the one above the astral level, but that 'White Arrow' would come from the higher level when the energies were right. Bernard was told that his wife was sitting next to him and laughing. Chi tried to explain about the energies, but it was a bit complicated.

Audrey came back, and after briefly asking us what we had got, the tape was played back and we then closed the circle and had a discussion over tea and flapjacks.

8/12/94 SA opened the circle. I tried to relax and clear my mind, but found it very difficult: had no visual images, but felt lots of energy around my head and 'around' generally. Chi came through after about fifteen minutes, very clearly and less trace of an accent. He referred to a message from White Arrow that the others knew about, and which he wished to discuss, or at least bring it to the knowledge of the entire group. There was great concern on the other side over the use of drugs, and the effect this was having on people's auras. These became 'sticky' and took a long time and a lot of effort to clear. He said that diseases such as Aids had little effect on the aura, but long-term use of drugs did. 'They' were becoming concerned about this problem and wished to draw it to our attention, wondering if it was possible to get the children starting on drugs to receive a sharp shock – letting them know what the effects could be. After a few questions from others, we agreed to discuss this afterwards.

Then he let the African 'Zimbala' through, a happy person with a big booming voice, who had lived in Botswana and had many, many wives and children! He discussed the disappearance of the animals in his native country, and agreed with Bernard that hunting animals should only occur if it was *necessary* to live. I got a mild reproof for not opening my mouth! The circle was closed and we had a long and interesting discussion on drugs and various other topics over tea and cake.

15/12/94 Despite feeling quite unwell, I did attend. We started with meditation, but I got no images or colours, but felt a presence and had the thought that there was a spirit in contact with each of us in the group.

Unexpectedly White Arrow came through – just for a short while, as the energy was limited. We had to project more and higher, as high as we could go. He mentioned that it was difficult to get through the layers down to us. We must get rid of 'bad' thoughts as quickly as possible, and try to give out as much peace and love to the world as we could. In answer to SA he said that we should keep to a closed circle. She also asked about the different advice and information from different spirits and circles –

he said that it depended on the level of the spirit, we must aim for the highest, and he wasn't the highest. Our group was there to learn as much as possible. Meditation was important, doing it often helped to clear the auras. Bernard asked about his earthly existence and he said that, yes, he had been a Red Indian, a shaman, but that he had been given permission not to incarnate again, but to progress further on that side. He left soon after that.

Audrey came back, and had a sore left eye for a short time, and was very thirsty. She commented that the experience was unusual – it was if she had no stomach! Then tea and cake and a lively talk, and we agreed to meet again on the 5th January 1995.

5/01/95 Stan absent due to illness. I was reasonably relaxed for the meditation but didn't go very deep. Audrey spoke: a Sister Anna came through, though very quietly and I think with some difficulty. She said she had been a nursing nun from the Sacred Heart order and worked in Gambia, where, together with other nuns and a doctor, she had been stopped on a mercy mission, surrounded by guerillas and then killed, shot through the throat. This had been in 1986. She liked the experience of coming through to us and had been attracted by our 'lights'. These had been nice colours, with a pink that gave harmony to them. Her emotions were still earthbound (perhaps this explained the difficulty in speaking). She wanted to continue healing, and perhaps we could think of her when we were giving out for healing.

White Arrow then came through and answered questions. Mike asked about humankind's first encounter with spirit, but didn't put it very well. White Arrow gave a lengthy reply involving other planets and beings, and that originally we didn't have to speak etc., but only think and it was done. However, as man became more materially conscious he lost much of his spiritual side. I asked about myths and legends and whether any of these referred to other planets etc., but he said that at least 90% of them had a historical basis on earth.

We were asked to help SA – and after some encouragement someone came through, but with very great difficulty. They didn't stay very long, but the channel had been opened, so presumably they will be back. White Arrow said that we must not tell others of these matters who are not yet ready to receive them. Also, we all had tasks to do, either as individuals or as a group, but that this had yet to be decided. We had started, but there was a long way to go yet.

12/01/95 Mike absent due to sore back, and this proved to be the last attendance by Stan. We had a short meditation before White Arrow came through. Using a clock, he said his world is very fast, like the second hand; the minute hand is like the astral world, much slower, and slower still is the material plane, like the hour hand. Then he suggested that we should not think of our universe as upright, but horizontal, like balls in water, the planets are round but in a flat plane – all is joined.

I asked about reincarnation. White Arrow declared that our soul's knowledge decides when to come back; many may come to teach or just to help. Some people, who are afraid of life and need a prop, are taught by souls who have come for that purpose (those who need to be taught patience or to accept illness, etc.). I then asked about the different levels. He replied first with the physical level, then the astral level which is very close to it, and from which we get inspiration and intuition. Then the emotional level, where we try to overcome our emotions as these hold you back. We must develop non-attachment. The emotional level is difficult for us, and it may take aeons of time for us to drop this connection with our emotional side. Then the mental level, where souls learn a great deal about the spiritual side of our being. This is where musicians, doctors, teachers and great thinkers always go after getting over the emotional barriers. After that there are many spiritual levels. As you go higher, all thoughts of the Earth plane drop away and you just become spirit and go towards the white light. Then he said that the world's problems were gradually getting better, but there are still the occasional eruptions – like pimples on a youth's skin!

Bernard then asked about Sai Baba. White Arrow reported that life is eternal; it does not stop when the body fades away. All souls eventually reach the white light. All will reach the Godhead. We all have lessons to learn. You cannot wipe out a soul. There have been many great teachers on your Earth plane, but that does not mean that any one of them was the Godhead. If you cannot accept something that you are told, that does not negate all the teaching – but question everything! All have a God divinity within you – look within yourself for the truth. "I will say no more about this person at the moment, until I find out more of this soul."

White Arrow said a little about Mike's back, and mentioned that SA "fought with herself". I asked about Sister Anna (from last week), who said that she wanted to continue with her healing work. I had thought about her on Monday [Healing Group] and wanted to know if she could possibly have been there. However, he remarked that he didn't know, as he is not on the same level, but he will find out.

Then he told us that things are going to change in our world. There may be unexpected passings and unexpected events, many passings all at once, individual passings that are not expected. Earth could be in turmoil, but this is needed because the Earth is going to go into a new phase. He said that he did not want us to be frightened – life is eternal – but things happen. People will gradually become more loving to each other but without so much of the emotional side. They will learn to give unconditional love, emotions will gradually fade away.

Bernard then mentioned a probable meteor strike in the southern half of the UK (23rd July 1999?). White Arrow stated that the Earth would not disappear – as such. Bernard asked what could we do, and the reply was to give unconditional love for the whole of our world, and realise that everything is as it should be. Fear is the greatest of the emotions that we must learn to conquer. *Always* remember the spirit *is* eternal. There is nothing in the universe that can kill the spirit, and that is the core of our being. "You can try to teach people this in your daily lives, if they cannot accept your teaching just send out love towards them. You cannot make anybody believe something unless that person is ready to receive it – but you can give them love."

He gave personal advice to two of the circle and went on to say: "If you drop the emotions you can think clearer. Use your heart centre. Keep down the emotional centre, your solar plexus centre. When you feel the emotions swelling up into the heart centre, think of your yellow solar plexus area going down – not up. It is from your love centre that all will be conquered, not from the emotional side. Love is something that you do for someone without the self. Give love anonymously, without any thought of reward. Then the problem of ego, you need a certain amount of ego to do things – but we have to regulate it. Try to drop the selfish side."

After talking to another in the circle he ended with, "Find knowledge wherever you can, just seek and accept what you can. I send you all love and light. Peace be with you."

19/01/95 Weather quite bad, but Mike, Audrey and myself made it to Bernard's. When White Arrow came through he asked for as much energy as we could give (the voice was quite soft to begin with). Sister Anna had not got over her death and was quite emotional, but she had to accept the killing. She was thankful to get through, and was now considering her options, either working directly with a human light or to work on the astral plane. She could come back through to the Earth plane but that needs lots of energy. She is still "fighting with herself". Sister Anna was a very loving human being and she cannot accept that people would want to do what they did to her.

I asked about the 'flat universe' talk of last week. He suggested it was like a bicycle, with gears and cogs; the chain connects them all so it can go on and on. All is connected.

I asked about the drugs again. He maintained that if drugs have been used only for a short period of time, this can be overcome and the aura restored, but it does depend on the length of time and the strength of these drugs. Other things don't affect the aura to the same extent as these drugs. With rest the aura can revive itself, but drugs give difficulties. Even brain damage can be easily overcome when it is 'normal' damage, but with drugs as well it gives trouble. Radiation is a problem, but not to the same extent. It gives an extra energy boost to the aura, but can be calmed down. It does not 'break' the aura and it does not go 'liquid' like the effects of drugs.

Man's understanding of the universe is limited. Human beings find it difficult to imagine how vast the universe is. We are all attached to the central 'hub' – where the chain of the 'bicycle' is. Scientists are astonished at some of the things they are finding out. You do not realise what your brains are capable of – it is possible to walk through walls and to go down to the bottom of your seas. Your mind can take you wherever you want to go. Out of body experiences – when they have learnt to control this they can turn themselves into any shape they want to be and go wherever they want to go. Only the physical body has limits.

Bernard asked about attachments to the Earth plane. White Arrow began by saying that the mind has been confined to the physical body and it has lost so much knowledge that it once had, etc., but that man once did not live so. Man has organised into cities etc., because it is easier. Man has become lazy, and there are now many attachments. Man turned his mind inwards instead of outwards; started thinking of himself, instead of being at one with nature, he turned round and decided that nature will work for him.

Bernard asked about loved ones meeting again. He said it depends on both your souls. If the other soul has passed over and 'it' agrees to stay to meet you, then you will meet. But the other soul may need to go on. "I will never say that you will never meet. I think that you will find that everyone will have someone to help them over. Many souls stay in the astral plane for aeons of time. If souls have got over the emotional side, they have jumped and then they have no need to meet. They may not meet up again for a few lifetimes. Many souls may come back to teach and to help."

Somebody mentioned group souls. "Group souls can come back for different reasons. If you have souls that have suffered greatly together, then they will meet up again on your earthly plane. If you have souls that decide they must teach, sometime during their lifetime they will meet again. There are different reasons for group souls. There are quite a few group souls at the moment coming down to teach and to help where it is needed. I find that the energy here … have we got a problem with our thoughts here? I feel that there is somebody here who is not happy with the contents of this information. The light is not so strong."

Bernard asked again about hunting, which was answered briefly. Then White Arrow enquired, "Would you mind if I called you the 'children of Light'? That is what we consider humans opening up to the higher forms. We see your lights. Unfortunately there are still far too many dark areas. It is very difficult to get through to people who have got such fixed ideas. Mostly the fault of religion. Try to spread the word. We know that it can be difficult, but we need every little seed that you can drop. Many things have got to be broken down. Do not lose heart if others go against you. Once you are on the path there is no turning back. The wider the path, the more souls will be opened.

"Every religious path has got to be broken down, there are only one or two exceptions. Even what you call Spiritualism is set in its ways. Many religious souls are not bad souls; it is just that they are on a path that will not take them very far. It is getting to the time when we need more souls to be turned towards the light. We do not wish now for the souls to keep on returning back to Earth, the time will come when they are needed to go towards the light."

There was then talk on stopping and the energy level. "Now that the contact has been made I can still come down, but yes, it is harder for both of us. It is not easy for the daughter of light. God bless to you all."

26/01/95 All five of us present. White Arrow came through, and Bernard opened the questions by asking about the spiritual path, how we can progress and about the obstacles. "It is only yourselves that stop this progress, you become too wrapped up in yourselves, over anxious, confused, and do not let the energies flow. People are at the point that they are, for different reasons. Sometimes they are needed to be at that particular point in their existence; sometimes they get so confused that they do not know which path to take. This is when they have to stop and look at themselves, and this is when they start to think: why am I here? What have I come for? And they have to sort themselves out. In a way it is a bit like string that is all tangled up. You have to sort it out and straighten it before you can make it workable."

Bernard asked if it was possible to accelerate along the path. "Oh yes! By giving yourselves unconditionally – it is as simple as that. You stop yourselves by your own behavior. You must remember that everybody is on their own paths and you have no right to interfere with that path unless that person wishes to proceed along it – then you can help.

"I have to bring myself back down to remember the different times that exist on Earth. It is a long time since I existed on the Earth plane and it is difficult for me."

Mike asked whether contemplation and meditation were valuable tools for progress. "Yes! They are very valuable. Meditation is a <u>very, very</u> valuable tool. You have to learn to let go in your meditation, to let all your preconceived ideas fall away from you, and just let be. Do not strain, do not worry if you don't receive a message or a light or anything in your meditation. This is part of the lesson, learning just to let go, and then after a time you will find that things will come to you. You will get in touch with the higher energies. But do not worry if you do not receive, for the lesson is learning to let go. But meditation is the key to progressing – if you give out your love to all. You cannot feel deep compassion for everyone, for there are some people that you will recognise that are on – shall we say – on a lower path, they have not proceeded very far, but you must send out as much love for them as you can."

I then asked about previous talks on the mind's ability to travel etc., and is this ability, that we once had, to be returned to us? "Yes, this is a facility shall I say, that humans have had, but have rejected and in aeons of time man became more self-centred and this produced heavier energies. Instead of looking outwards to other humans, they started to look within themselves only, and this facility was gradually taken away – or put aside. But like the sleeper it is still there and it only needs reawakening for you to be able to do it again."

Mike asked about 'man's fall' in this respect, why did he change? "He changed because what he saw on Earth was good, and he made a conscious effort of taking to himself the things that he liked and surrounded himself with these things, and over aeons of time this made the energies within him heavier. It is a little like taking up a heavy stone. It weighs you down, but once you drop the stone you become lighter, and you can run faster."

Mike then said, "We were on a heavy vibration and adopted a heavier one for selfish reasons?" White Arrow replied, "Yes! You see not every being was like this; this is where you had the forces of what you described as good and evil. There were people that still realised that by doing this it kept you down; though over time, shall I say 90% of the people became heavier. There are even today some beings that can still do this. You do not hear of them because they don't want to get contaminated, they will not let the rest of the world know that they have the ability to do this.

"As regards going forward on the path my friend; if you can just let go of yourself, just let it fall away. It is rather like when you sleep at night, you relax and let go, and you have no real conscious knowledge of that, that last point between being awake and being asleep, that you are there – is this correct? [Yes.] You have gone over into the dream state without realising. So if you say, 'I'm here, use me', and relax and let go. You must realise children of Light, that you all here have started on that pathway, you are not being held back, and once you are on that pathway there is no turning back. Do not get frustrated. You will go along that pathway until you reach the very point where you will turn to light. What is your frustration at this very moment?"

Bernard said it was the thought of all those wasted years in the past, and that he had to try to make up for them now. "Those years, dear friend, are *not* wasted. It is a part of your lesson. Without you going through that period you would not have realised the things that you have had to learn. There is not a thing that happens that is wasted – it is all a part of the lesson. You can only live for the moment. I think that you all begin to realise that there is no past and no future, there is only the moment that you live in."

Mike asked about the astral plane. "It is possible that some souls are so advanced that they only need a very short period of time on the astral plane, before they go on to the much higher planes of thought and spiritual awareness. Most souls do rest on the astral plane for some time, to wash off the heaviness of your Earth plane. It is a plane of recuperation and of learning, but for advanced souls, they only use it to recuperate and so go on to the higher planes."

I then asked about whether when going from one plane to another we experience similar 'death' as we do on leaving the Earth plane. "Yes, for on the astral plane your minds are still very much like they are here on Earth for the normal spirits. ["My goodness!" from SA] May I reassure you that you do not feel pain on the astral plane. There is no day or night, it is light all the time, but it is still a place of learning. What one has to learn depends on one's spirit."

SA asked about the many passings. "There is a purpose for many passings. I am not at liberty to divulge much information on this. They are needed for different things, for different work to be done."

Bernard asked if there was a choice in the work we undertake or whether we are directed. "Yes, you are given a choice, but in the end you will realise yourself that what is asked of you is the right path for you. There is no pressure on the individual soul; it is for that soul to come to individual enlightenment. Are you happy with the explanation? [Yes.] There is no point in me coming if I cannot enlighten you in some way.

"Things have got to be broken down. People that are glimpsing the knowledge in a very minor way, have got to be enlightened that there is more to the spirit world than just getting messages from friends and loved ones – it has got to be opened up – that is all very well, but it is not the true course of things, you are only making small pinpricks. It has got to be split open and the truth of the knowledge has got to be put out to all the people that are at that point, to accept the knowledge. This is where I said before; do not get disheartened when you get rebuked. You must have faith in your beliefs. You must stand firm – but also show love and compassion. It always comes down to love. Do not judge others for what they do. I realise that your world is self-centred and that many turn this into hatred for other souls. I can assure you this will change.

"It must be very difficult for you to realise that it will change. And it is the children of Light, yourselves, that help to make this change. The lights are getting more and more over your world, are beginning to spread, so that it will make one glorious light, the energies are being sent down.

"I have a soul with me now, who has progressed greatly. He was very well known on your Earth plane, and at sometime, sometime, he would like to introduce to you as he was known. This will be on some other occasion.

"May I say, as I think as I said once before, that you are all capable of receiving your guides through yourselves. Just let your ego drop away, for it is only your egos that are stopping you. We so desperately need your friends to come through so you yourselves can experience and realise, so you can go out on your own and carry the message further. I will go now. I send you all love and light, you children of Light. Bless you all."

2/02/95 All five of us present. White Arrow came through and asked us to play some music before we even started. Now that Stan had left, we had discussed getting a replacement, and Mike asked White Arrow about this. "Whoever it is that you ask, must be open, must want to come for their own development, for their own sake. It is no good asking someone and they will accept, without them feeling that, as they have been asked, they have to attend. I am sure that you will know the right person, by all means ask. She, yourselves and I will know."

Then to SA, "Our friend must not be afraid to talk!" Mike suggested that she was having doubts, afraid that it was clairvoyance and not direct voice. "This does not matter. You must realise, that whatever you are given is meant to be. It is not you; it has been given to you to give. She must put away her own doubts, whatever comes into her mind ... we will not let her give out any information that is not correct or not appropriate. I think that when this new spirit to your group does eventually come through, you will all be very surprised. Dear children of Light, you must have faith. It is good to question, it is good to enquire, but never close the door entirely on things that are delivered to you.

"We do realise that you are all struggling with your own consciences, and beliefs that have been pumped into you throughout your existences, and it takes time to break down these beliefs. We have patience, we know that it will come about and we are looking to you to spread the word. This is not done quickly. Like seeds that are planted in the ground, you place them in the appropriate place where they will get nourishment, where they will get watered, where the roots will grow strong, and the plants will grow healthy towards the light. This cannot be done on rocky ground. You must have the right conditions, the right soil to plant that seed."

Mike then asked about releasing this information. "Yes! It is like a tap. You turn the tap on slowly and give it out slowly, let it out little by little. Do not turn the tap on full. You must have patience and do it slowly. Put it into the hands of the people you feel can accept this knowledge."

SA then said that the person trying to get through was called 'White Smoke', and was on the same level of White Arrow. The latter then reported, "We are a Brotherhood. Whenever you find 'white', we are all on the same level. Does this please you? [Yes.] Do not be afraid. Do not hold back. You are frightened it is your own mind. Please let him come." Mike then asked if it was a question of lowering ones consciousness just a fraction more, so that one was relaxed enough to allow the spirit to come. "That's right! This is what I have been trying to impress on you all. The letting go! When you are in a circle as you are now, there is safety. You have put protection around yourselves. We have seen your lights. We do not allow the lower vibrations, entities, to enter. Please let him come through, as he has been with you for a long time. Do not worry about your own thoughts for we have to use the human body to get our message over. Will you relax and let go?"

Then White Smoke spoke through SA: "My light has come through.

Willow Circle

There are many plants, but like the lily the roots are in damp soil and have taken a while to grasp. The bloom is not quite here, but the plant itself is nourishing that flower, and the bud *will* open. When it opens it will be blue and very beautiful. It is necessary to sit in the light for this process to take place. My friend needs to leave, to take a step aside and allow me to come through. Tonight she has put herself in a boat. I am pleased that now I am allowed to come forward. Each of you must listen and practice in the same method. Each of you has a guiding light. Each from the Brotherhood, who has come each night with you; you must set aside your thoughts. This is difficult with so much technology, but it is the only way."

White Arrow: "We are pleased with her now!"

White Smoke: "There are many more people, but I fear it will be longer before we can allow them to come through."

Bernard then asked about the rest not being ready.

White Smoke: "You are ready too! You must let go. It takes practice. Perhaps you need a spell between you all where you just let go, and forget what else is happening in the room. Forget trying the communication, concentrate on letting go. Practice that, this will make it much easier."

White Arrow: "May I say it is a little like lying on a bed in the sun. Let your body absorb the sunlight, you are completely relaxed."

White Smoke: "This is also not easy. Many have difficulty in doing such a simple task. To completely let go only happens in rare moments. Capture those moments; take them to your mind. Remember how this feels and emulate this when you sit in the circle." White Smoke then remarked on the constant fidgeting by Mike, before leaving. SA thanked White Arrow for his help, and he replied that he was so pleased that she let go. Mike said "One down and three to go!"

"We all like laughter, it raises the vibrations. Laughter is the source of life. Just let go. I know the male gender finds it much more difficult than the female gender. There are male and female genders in every human being. If there wasn't you would be unbalanced, the male would be so hard and the female too soft. You have to have this balance within you. So you males – let that female side of you come out a bit more! Let it go!" Mike then asked what if spirit came through all of us? "Then we will have a party!"

White Arrow then went on to say that Sister Anna was very happy now, and that she had made a breakthrough. She has a lot of work to do. She needed to touch the Earth plane again as she did. She loved babies and young children and was now surrounded by them!

"God bless you all now. Go out children of Light. Go in peace and harmony and walk with spirit." Then right at the very end: "I have just been told before I go – this is a clue – look for Trafalgar Day."

Then we had tea, cakes and much discussion.

9/02/95 All five of the circle present. Chi came through first, saying that somebody had wished to come through to us, but that Chi had to disallow it as he would have brought his earthly condition with him, and that this would not have been good for 'my lady'. He was going to delay him until he could control his emotions. [Audrey later said that at the start she had some very strange and sore feelings around her heart area] Then Chi gave Audrey and Mike advice about Chinese characters and writing, that they needed to get a decent book to do it from – with information on arm and hand movements etc.

White Arrow came through: "I wish to give you each a rose of love. But I wish to give the female gender a bunch of flowers. This is for work that has been done and also for [to SA], you feel very low and your light is not shining like it should. You will take these flowers and smell the perfume, and these flowers will enrich your senses and lift your spirits – for they are heavenly flowers. They are given in love. Are there any questions?"

Bernard then asked about apports, saying that the present company had never seen them. "Are you asking for an apport?" Bernard said yes – if that is not the wrong thing to do, but if it is then no. "You see, you all have gifts. Each one of you have a gift, but you have not got, in this little circle, the person that can receive the apport." Bernard said he fully understood. I let it go, but will have to ask Bernard about it. "But of course you never know! You may be surprised!"

Bernard asked if it was alright to know what our gifts were. "As I have said previously, this circle has the gift of being able to have our spirit friends come through. Each and every one of you has this gift. You have also got the gift of healing within this circle. The gift is what we consider the greatest gift. When you have apports, these are just to show what we can do, and as a spectacular thing for human beings to see, and also to have faith in the spirit world. But it is only like a showpiece, it does not mean much. It is done only for effect. It is like larger circles (clairvoyant meetings)… it is only like a trinket."

I then asked about having protection when one was on ones own. "This is a matter of how deep you want to go. You must be very careful that you do not let yourself drift off too far. But as a matter of protection it is very good to ask for the very highest of the spirits to give you protection, to surround you with light. You must always ask for the very highest. Doing this, it is like a shield that is surrounding you, that will not allow any of the lower, uneducated vibrations, to come through.

"There are many different ways of doing this, and I personally feel it is for yourself to find the way that you are most comfortable with. But always remember, whatever way you decide to do this – you must surround yourself from under your feet to the top of your head. You must make sure that it goes all the way round. You must not leave out the bottom of your feet – that is so important. But please ask for the very high. If you ask for any of the White Brotherhood, they will give you protection." Mike asked about the Brotherhood. "It is just a term for you earthlings! We have no gender. We are all on the same level. We are pure spirit."

Bernard asked whether we had any awareness of knowledge from a previous life in our new incarnation. "You have awareness of it. All things must be broken down now. Because this knowledge is shut tight from babyhood in many cases. But you all come through with a particular character: you may be aggressive, gentle, thoughtful for others, selfish, etc. It s all within your character. You may wish to go along a certain pathway. You know instinctively within yourselves what is right and wrong. Brothers and sisters may have completely different characters. The person who is gentle has learnt from a previous lifetime, and it is written within his character."

Bernard said: "So it is for the cruel one to right what is wrong?" "Yes! The thing is with so many people, that the parents will lead the children along a path that may not be the correct path. But because the child believes the parents, then it is easy for the child to follow – until they get to a certain age when they can decide for themselves. It is much easier to go on one journey where they don't have to think of what is right or wrong."

SA asked if there were other factors such as peer group and culture etc.

"Yes. When you get a very sensitive person in amongst a peer group, then that sensitive person has learnt that lesson and he finds it very hard. They may torment him, they will call him all kinds of names, but that person knows deep down within them that that group is not doing the right thing. This is where I mean it is so easy to follow. If you get somebody who is slightly weak in character; even though he knows he is doing wrong he wants to follow that peer group, because he thinks they are better than him, or there is something in that group that he wants, so he goes along with them. This group will seize on a person like that and they will make him do things that he knows really it is wrong to do. It is very easy to get led astray, along a wrong line. This is where the person will stand still and not go any further, or will have to come back again, perhaps with a slightly different character to help them. As you know, you all have got different characters, you all think slightly differently. So in groups you may basically think alike, but you all have thoughts of your own, and some people will sit back and let others dominate."

There was then a break of about a minute. "I was taken away for a particular purpose. There was something I had to do." White Arrow then went on to say that character lessens as one gets nearer the light – essentially it is dealt with on the emotional plane. However, when we are reincarnated we are given certain strengths to help us along that path.

Mike then asked about whether it is preordained that certain 'horrible' characters came into the world like that. "There always has to be the balance in between the two. Because your world has decided aeons back that that is the way it would be. But it does not always have to be like that; it does not have to be like that in the future. It is gradually getting better. … Ego … Most people who start out with 'good', can get a big ego, and think that they know what is best for the world."

SA then talked about the fear of the ego taking over, and there was a general debate with Mike and Bernard. However, I thought that SA was quite negative and became sharp with White Arrow, who asked her to reflect on what had been said. "Perhaps the flowers will help. Your strengths are given to combat your weaknesses. Look at yourselves. Note what you feel your strengths are and what your weaknesses are, and then realise that those strengths are being given to you to overcome those weaknesses, to support you, to hold you up as you go along life's highway.

I send you all love and light. It is only that you are true of heart that you doubt, my friend!"

Then tea and cake!

16/02/95 Just four of us, SA is ill. Started with a meditation that seemed to last for a long time. I felt lots of facial and hand sensations, but found it difficult to still the mind. When White Arrow did come through he was very faint, and there was an air of sadness about his voice. "I've been waiting to see if any of you will allow your friends to come through. I open myself to you. Is there anything I can inform you of in any way?"

Mike then said that we were trying to let them through and was there anything we could do to help this. "I have tried to explain how you can do this before. They are so much with you. But I have been holding back. There is sorrow here tonight." Mike then explained about SA and her illness. "That is why I gave her a big bunch of flowers. I have been thinking that I may withdraw for a period, over your next few meetings, so our instrument may watch you and help draw the other friends closer."

Mike asked if there was any other way we could begin our circle. "It is good to meditate before you sit to develop. If it is possible to have a period of time to meditate before you start to open up to spirit. This is a great help, and also the music is also a great help. You do not have to be quiet in your meditations. If you have vibrations that will help you raise…" Mike: "Can we use a little taped music to relax ourselves?" White Arrow replied: "Yes. Any that you all find harmonious. This is a good vibration. I will withdraw, for I know Chi has a friend who wishes to come through. Blessings on you all. Do not allow your spirits to become too low, for we are here to help you. Things will go well. We will send you strength and love, and please believe all will be well."

Chi came through, saying that a young fellow, who had been very persistent to come through, was waiting. We then heard 'Joe': "Hello me old cock sparrow!" A cockney, who lived and worked in the London docks in Stepney at the time of Queen Victoria. He didn't have a wife. He worked on the barges, lighterman, and enjoyed the work. He died young – in fact he was murdered by two men who came at night to steal. He didn't know about them, and interrupted them. They slugged him around the head and shoved him into the water. "Got away with it they did." He had a little dog called Jack, a white and brown terrier, a good ratter. He loved his dog, which was still with him. He didn't know any parents, had no surname, and he survived when young by begging, then lived rough or occasionally some friends would put him up. He told us that he didn't do much now, not like he used to. "I just saw the light and thought it would be nice to go." He wanted to come back. Never seemed to have been away from the dock area, as he said he didn't know Trafalgar Square or Charring Cross. He left with a "Ta-ta then."

Chi then said that Joe had asked if he could come back and we all agreed that he could. Chi ended the meeting: "We all send our greetings to you all."

23/02/95 This was a bit of a surprise! Apparently SA had expressed doubts about what she had been getting, and about 'what' was coming through Audrey. Therefore she contacted DS and arranged that he attend tonight (presumably from her previous group). I thought this was a bit much, but didn't want to bring any disharmony to the proceedings. So six were in attendance.

DS's spirit friends came through him, always referring to 'themselves' as 'we'. They asked that we use our critical faculties, and question and examine everything that spirit says; either accept it or discard it. You should have full conscious control over your body at all times. You have the right to say no, or to say to spirit to wait or come back at another time, etc. You have free will. Spirit must respect an individual's free will. Spirit will ask an individual's permission to use them as an instrument. Your critical faculty will protect you from lower planes. Use caution, seek proof. Do not *ever* believe any spirit – test first. We have to take things slowly, step by step – we would grow. Take your time – you have eternity. Do not be disheartened; you are on the right track, etc.

Apart from stating some obvious things, I'm not sure what this was meant to achieve. There was an inference that SA thought that White Arrow was 'suspect', that he used fear. If this was the case, why not let White Arrow come through and question him? However, this was not done. This will need to be discussed by the group, but SA is away on holiday next week. We had tea and cake, and DS seemed a pleasant enough person.

9/03/95 With SA on holiday there were just four of us. We started with Audrey in charge and the rest of us trying to let go. I found it difficult (as usual) to stop my mind from working overtime. However, very relaxing, with 'feelings' on my head, face and hands. Mike very nearly got a breakthrough, but Audrey spoke at just the wrong time!

Next we swapped, and after a while Chi came through Audrey, and announced that he had brought a jade vase for us and had put it on the table. Green jade with a brown bit in it, decorated with flowers and three birds; Audrey was to paint it sometime.

Bernard asked about homosexuals! Chi replied that the West was preoccupied with sex; it was the spirit that counted. We all had male and female inside us, and it was at birth that our sexual inclinations were decided. But – as the same with colour – it was the person 'inside', the spirit that mattered. A few other things were discussed, and Bernard asked after his wife, etc., before we ended. Chi reminded us about the music, which we had forgotten to play before starting.

We had a long discussion over tea and biscuits. I am now fully 'back' with the group, having had seeds of doubt trouble me. However, it has been a good learning and reflective exercise. I suggested we should always start with a 30 minutes meditation before Audrey 'relaxed'.

16/03/95 All five of the group present. We decided on the half hour meditation at the start. I found it hard to settle and 'came out' early. Audrey was the last to come back, well over 45 minutes. I didn't like this aspect, as she was supposed to watch over us! However, spirit did not come through, so we closed and had tea and cake. No mention of SA's past objections! Not sure how this group is going forward.

23/03/95 All present. Everybody seemed to be slightly healthier than in previous weeks! Started with meditation, and I got a 'twitch' or sudden jerk close to the start of it, but relaxed more later. However, I was always conscious of my back, right side, and after 30 minutes I got my 'sensation' that jerked me awake at once. The rest came out after about 10 minutes. Zimbala came through, but not very jolly or very strong. He stayed only a short time. So we closed the meeting and had tea and cake.

Then SA announced that she was thinking of attending another development circle, and so would now leave ours. This came not unexpectedly, but with a bit of relief by me – the circle could not have continued as it was, as there was not the harmony that is required. I think Bernard is worried about getting replacements, but the rest of us agreed that things should take their course naturally.

30/03/95 Full complement of four present. I thought that it was a much better atmosphere. Meditation was not very deep, waiting for my 'spasm' to come, which it did on about the half hour. The others seemed fine.

Chi came through saying that there were holes to repair in our cloth! When Mike said that we had a lady in mind, Chi told us to treat her with kid gloves and to go slowly with her. He reported that there were others waiting to come through, but he would not let any come, as there was so little power. Joe had tried to slip his dog through and come after – but was prevented. Chi disclosed that Joe would soon be reincarnated. He also told Mike and Audrey much about their dogs – past and present – and told Bernard that his were with him. Lastly he said that we had to be like the wise owl and wait, listen, look, learn, and when we were ready, then we would 'pounce'.

My 'side' still bothering me and affecting my general demeanour – as well as my meditations. If after the holidays it has not improved I may have to go to the doctor.

13/04/95 All present plus two of Bernard's relatives. Good warm atmosphere. Chi came through saying that the 'lights' were wonderful and that he had a jade bead for each of us. He asked if we had any news on the drugs issue, but we could not help him. He announced that White Arrow would come through when the energy levels had built up. Then he went on to say various things to the others that had come up at the last circle – which I had missed.

Chi then let Joe come through. Joe told us that his dog Jack was with him and talked a little about his last life. He had often been helped by the prostitutes when he was young, often getting a 'Stepney bun' (which was full of fruits) to eat. He used to pinch fruit, etc., from the market, along with a few pals. He had now taken up woodcarving and was really liking it.

Chi came back to round it off before we closed.

Willow Circle

20/04/95 All present. Didn't think that Audrey would come as she has not been well, but she did, though looked a bit 'distracted'. I had brought the Chinese music tape to play for Chi, though I'm not sure if it helped the meditation! We sat for nearly an hour, but nobody came through. My back held up well, still getting the sensation on my right side but at least the spasms have stopped. Had tea and cake – at the insistence of Bernard – who recounted the laughs he had during the war.

27/04/95 Only Bernard and myself, as the others are ill. Had meditation for about 50 minutes. Then a good chat over tea and biscuits.

4/05/95 Bernard, Mike and myself. Had the meditation, then tea and cake, plus talk of politics!

11/05/95 All present. Meditation to music, and then after some time Chi came through: "Good evening. I don't intend to stay long as my lady and I have not been very well. I have just come to say if you look back over the period of time that you have been sitting, how things have gone on, have been 'knocking', and you have been tested.

"Now comes the period, like the ebbing tide, when all will be calm. It is a time to reflect and a time to gather your strengths, for you will need them. For as I have said before, there is much work for you to do. You must all gather your strengths. Ask for as much help as you think is needed, we will always be here to help. But you must work yourselves. Calmly, but with the knowledge that we are here to give you advice. You must not think that you are not worthy. We do need you very much. Gather the strength within yourselves and be ready. Spend time each day getting in touch with us. Things will not happen quickly – but when they do they will explode. But we are waiting for you *all* to get strong. The testing time is over. I will send you all blessings. Be happy. *Be* happy.

"You have knowledge now of the spirit world. Just have clear thoughts. I think that you all will be surprised. There will be other people that will be surprised as well! If you sit and meditate and think, and give yourselves over completely to the knowledge that we can supply you with – it will be like drinking a cup of pure gold. Our blessings go out to you all. We will meet again."

18/05/95 All present. A long period of meditation, with music at the start. After roughly 45 minutes, Chi came through. He said we had to have somebody in charge of the circle and awake, as there had been quite a traumatic experience. They were taking part in a 'rescue' and, "My lady is rather taken aback by the situation. The situation has been partly dealt with. You will know this person – everybody knows this person – he has been earthbound for quite a few of your years. I will just say that his name is 'John'. I should also like to say, look out for a big lady to join your circle, or rather a 'well made' lady! I will leave you and I will try to avoid this happening again."

Bernard then asked what we should do if this ever occurred again. We were to ask the entity to be at peace and to calm down, that they are with friends and that they may talk to you or turn to see the light. Or they may need to rest – you will have to judge the situation. "I was not very vigilant! He came in very quickly and got through me, it was so sudden. Blessings on you. You must be vigilant. Till we meet again. Look for the big lady!"

When Audrey came round, she said that her mouth was suddenly filled with blood, she was choking (She had coughed a few times) and her head felt numb. She had asked for help and then for a name, she got 'John'. When she asked when this had happened he said yesterday. Then she saw the motorcade and realised that this was J. F. Kennedy. Audrey said he was very agitated and panicky.

We discussed what had happened and Bernard said we must have a person in charge, and all questions must be put through him initially, as everybody talking drains the power of the circle. He also thought that our purpose in this circle was 'rescue' work. We agreed with most of that, though I was not so sure about the last bit.

25/05/95 All present, even though I had been feeling quite ill, I had decided to chance it. Mike played 'Zen Meditation' music, and the meditation was better than I expected. Felt that I had 'let go' just for a little while. Chi came through and gave us all a rose quartz crystal vase, which he placed on the table. Mike asked about Joe and was told that he was very happy and was learning slowly. Mike also asked about help for disasters and crashes etc. Chi replied that we should send out our prayers to help these souls. "Your world has so much information thrown at you, it is easy to dismiss it as just another accident, etc. But send out your thoughts for people that are passed, and these are picked up, the help will be there."

Chi then observed that we had not found our lady yet for the circle, but we all knew her and had passed her over! Later he said that he wanted to impress on us that we must learn to think positively about people. "Do not judge. It is so easy to think that you are right and they are wrong. And every negative thought makes the situation even more negative. It is not for you to judge someone else's situation. You must be positive, for there is so much negativity in your world. I will emphasise the fact that you have work to do. This has been stated before. When this other person comes into your circle there will be a big burst of energy and things will begin to happen."

Then more intriguing comments about the other person! Her name had been mentioned but rejected, etc. Chi said that he did not want to put thoughts into our minds, we had to realise for ourselves. "I will give you a week!" Then interestingly, "You know all human beings have bad habits." Next several animals came forward, cats and dogs, including Bernard's springer spaniel 'Bonzo'.

"Everything that you do on the Earth plane is recorded. I could say that it is a little like when you go to school – 'could do better'! When you get to the point when you do not prejudge other people, then you are on your way to understanding what you call the spirit world. I will say farewell now. I will just say before I go, don't think that you have been deserted by White Arrow, for this is not so.

"And your lady is patiently waiting for you." Bernard thought that this was for him, but it was for me! When I said that I was not sure what he was talking about, Chi said, "I believe you were shown a drawing – is this not so? She has a great deal of patience! I believe you have an opportunity to go to some lectures – take it." When Mike asked if Chi was addressing this to him, he was told, "To all of you. Blessings on you all." Then tea and cake, and a lot of thinking on my part.

1/06/95 All present. Audrey stayed 'awake' for the meditation to a Michel Jarre tape. Lots of energy around my head and eyes etc. Did have difficulty in really relaxing and so being able to let go, but felt I was improving. Very briefly saw a face on its side with eye closed, this opened and then it all faded. Also a few colours but little else. Got 'rocked' a few times and didn't know if this was a signal to 'wake up' or something else. Heard Bernard fidgeting and Audrey moving, so opened my eyes to see that Mike was very deep. Audrey talked to him, but got no response, and Bernard put the music off suddenly and Mike came back soon after – but it looks very promising. Bernard had felt lots of energy and had 'heavy' arms. As only 40 minutes had passed, we decided to go again, but without the music.

Soon, Chi came through and said that he could not tell us who to pick to fill our circle – we had to decide that ourselves! Then he said that he had a little girl here – Anne Murray – aged nine and a half, and that her mother (who is still living) knew my mother. She herself had passed over about two years ago. I said I would enquire. [I did get in touch with my mother, but she couldn't remember anybody of that name.]

Chi told Bernard to look out for a morning sunrise. After a few other things he said, "Simplicity is the key to all things." He told us that we had too much clutter in our lives and that we should in effect get down to basics. He also mentioned that we didn't ground ourselves properly. I asked for advice and was told to imagine extensions from the feet and the spine – extend the spine deep into the earth and also through the feet.

He closed soon after saying White Arrow had not forgotten us but was holding back to assist another of the White brotherhood to come through (Mike?).

8/06/95 All present. Meditation with Audrey keeping watch! After twenty minutes I heard Audrey and opened my eyes to find both Mike and Bernard 'away'. Mike wasn't as deep as last week and soon came out of it, as did Bernard. However, it looks very promising. We went again, but nothing this time, though I was more relaxed. Tea and cake and a beautiful sunset.

15/06/95 All present. Meditation with Audrey keeping watch again. I was better this time, but still can't keep the mind from working overtime! Mike and Bernard nearly away again after thirty minutes. There was then a chat for about fifteen minutes, describing their experiences. We had another go, with Mike keeping watch. I felt I was much deeper this time. I got pink colours and then a deep burgundy with a vague blue 'blob', but it did not turn into anything. I really wanted to keep at it, but heard the other two moving and shifting and watching me etc., which made me come out. However, I feel I have made a little first step.

Audrey said that she felt White Arrow and Chi were there, but were holding back, probably to let us move forward in our efforts. Audrey said that she got a voice that said something like 'your names will be written in the sands of time'. This took her back a bit and 'woke' her up! Tea and cake and a lovely sunset yet again.

22/06/95 All present. As before, first meditation with Audrey awake and second with Mike awake. The first one went ok. Found myself tensing up again after I had relaxed! Bernard felt a woman's presence (his wife) and had a few other experiences, but no breakthrough! The second meditation was better, and a few seconds before Audrey spoke; I felt a real calm and a sense of light. It was White Arrow, but he only stayed a very short time, as I think the energy level from us was very poor.

He gave us a symbolic message of light on a lily pad – it looks as if is floating in the air – but it is supported by a complex geometric pattern of its roots, which are embedded in the mud. This was like the Earth and the planets of the solar system, all are supported by a complex pattern (of energy?). Also I suppose, we are all linked with these forces. He sent us blessings, falling in a silver shower. He left soon after saying that the instrument was not feeling too well.

We closed and had tea and cake, and Bernard talked about the war. He also showed us his 'plane' that he had built (lots of work!) which he hopes to sell for charity.

29/06/95 All present. Mike and Audrey were a few minutes late. They were obviously a little irritable with each other, which stance they kept up all evening! Meditation was ok. Fairly shortly into it I suddenly felt really great and saw a disc of yellow, but it faded after a bit, though some other colours came. Felt a tingling around my eyes – but not round my head as usual. Quite relaxed, but I couldn't go any deeper. Mike seemed on the verge again, but Audrey was 'distracted' and didn't get deep enough, not even on the second go.

Think I may take a board, paper and pencil next time, something may come of it. Had tea and cake and Mike and Audrey argued!

6/07/95 All present. I brought a tape that we used for the meditation. I seemed to go towards sleep rather than anything else, and eventually got a spasm up my back again, and my side also felt funny. However, got the feeling of 'spiders webs' around my head again. Mike was supposed to keep watch, but he was away when I came out of my stupor after 30-40 minutes. However, just when I thought that nothing would happen like last week, White Arrow spoke: "Good evening. I have come this evening to have a short discussion on the elements and the changes of energies within your solar system. Energies have been changing now for the last hundred years, that is why there has been so much turmoil within your Earth. The energies have filtered down now to your physical level and now there are changes within your body patterns. These are necessary for the leap that will take place. Not all essential beings will make this leap to the higher realms, but those that do not will be sent to another plane, very much like yours, but it is on a higher, lighter wave than the density of your Earth plane.

"The turmoil within your world has been the result of peoples karma. Children are being born into your world now that have a different energy rate. These children are here to expel the rest of their karma – the little that they need to get rid of. These children will be the advance guard into the higher realms. You have nought to fear.

"Those of you who have no understanding will go along on their merry way. Those that are on the brink of the next big link will find the light so brilliant and so wonderful. We ask you children of Light, to help wherever you can, to smooth the way, to help as many souls to make that connection. There are many souls here, and souls that do not realise that they are working hard, that their higher selves have got the connection with us. They are good people, but in a mental and physical level they do not understand, but their higher selves are helping.

"We ask you all to be like the Good Shepherd and to help wherever you can, for the light years will not be long. I will say fear not, but be joyful. The harmony that you may hear is the harmony of the higher reaches.

"I will leave you now. I bathe you all in golden light and ask you to go forth. I will return very soon. Be of good cheer and know that all is as it should be. All is well."

Then tea and cake.

13/07/95 All present. Meditation to 'Redman' tape. Too many thoughts going through my head, and *again* I forgot to ground myself! Projected my higher chakras and concentrated on linking the circle (*Again* no one had been delegated to watch.). I felt that presence (and White Arrow) was there for some time, and was beginning to think that none would come through, when White Arrow spoke: "Good evening. I have been observing you. I would like to continue for a little while with what we were discussing the last time we met – the energies that are being passed down into your Earth planes and your bodies. It is like the singing of the universe. Each of you has your own song. There are some that will hear and some that will not.

"Do not be afraid if you become unbalanced in your head for a time. This I mean by off-balance. And if your extremities feel a buzzing within them, well this is all a part of the new energies that are descending. There are points within your body where they are being directed. They are behind your head, in the lower area of the skull. The main beam is where your skull joins the spine. There are two lower down each side and eventually there will be two higher up within your skull. Thus making what you would call an 'H'.

"Your Earth vibrates and is alive. As you must realise it is like a heartbeat forever pounding. The Earth has been a planet of learning. It is the most beautiful planet – but, unfortunately, you human beings take the negative. All this will change, as the Earth shifts so will the vibrations within your planet.

"As I have said previously, those that have seen the light will experience a beautiful transition. We do not prophesy when this will be; just know that it will be. We do not want to spread doom and gloom, for this is not what it is all about. You appreciate that we do not see time in the way that you see time. We have no concept of time as on your plane. All we say is that this will take place. So you sensitive ones, if you feel these feelings within your bodies, be joyful, for you know that you have made the connection with the universe and the song of the universe.

"I will leave you to mull this over. This is not a message to be depressed about, but to be joyful, to know in your very souls that life is eternal and that there are greater things ahead – things that you have no concept of. Joy be unto you all. I send you the eternal love. We will meet again."

There was quite a pause and then Chi came through: "Good evening. I have just come to let Joe have his last word. He will tell you."

Joe: "Hallo there!"
Circle: "Hallo Joe."
Joe: "I've come to say goodbye."
Circle: "That was nice of you."
Joe: "Yeah, I thought I'd say goodbye to you. They're sending me on a journey."
Circle: "Oh really?"
Joe: "Yeah. And I want to thank you for it's because of you that I'm going on this journey."
Circle: "Our pleasure. Who sends you on your journey, other teachers?"
Joe: "Yeah."
Circle: "Do you know where you are going?"
Joe: "No! I don't know!"
Circle: "It will be a surprise."
Joe: "Well my teacher who taught me woodwork, you know, the one that taught me to make boats? He said that I'm ready now to go on."
Circle: "Good. After having made the connection here?"
Joe: "Yeah. Don't know what I'm going to find though! Don't know what I'm going to do either."
Circle: "I'm sure you 'll be instructed."
Joe: "Yeah. I don't know if I can take Jack with me though."
Circle: "Why?"
Joe: "He said perhaps he couldn't come with me. I'm going to missJack."
Circle: "He'll wait for you. Do they say that you have to go on this journey?"
Joe: "They say I'm ready to go."
Circle: "Have you asked them if you could take Jack?"
Joe: "Yeah, and he said he didn't think he would be able to come with me. So I didn't know if I wanted to go or not, not being able to take Jack. But they said that if I went I would benefit from it. So I thought about it."
Circle: "I'm sure Jack will be in good hands."
Joe: "Oh Yeah!"

Circle: "We all wish you well, it's been smashing having you."
Joe: "I really enjoyed talking to you."
Circle: "We've enjoyed talking to you very much."
Joe: "Bye then."
Circle: "Goodbye, good luck."
Joe: "Ta-ta."
Circle: "God bless." [Pause]
Joe: "Don't want to go!"
Circle: "It's hard saying goodbye. Perhaps we may see you in our future. Perhaps we might have you back to tell us something about your journey in times to come. We'd like that."
Joe: "Yeah. I'd like that too."
Circle: "Perhaps you could bear that in mind."
Joe: "Yeah. Ta!"
Circle: "Ask your teacher if that's possible."
Joe: "Yeah, I'll ask him." [Then sadly] "Well, goodbye then."
Circle: "Goodbye Joe. Good luck."
Chi: "He has said his goodbyes. We will talk about Joe another time. I will let you know what he is doing. I do not think that he will be here for very long. I mean that he will be getting ready again for reincarnation. It will not be yet."
Mike: "This is preparation for it?" Chi: "Yes. That of course is why he cannot take his little dog with him. I will leave you. I thought my lady has had enough."
Tea and biscuits.

20/07/95 All present. Feeling quite ill, my innards bubbling away! No music. Couldn't relax into any meditation and got my 'spasm' twice. Also realised that yet again we hadn't agreed to who would keep watch! Had no feeling that White Arrow was there, but thought that maybe Chi would come. However, after 45 minutes or so, this 'entity' ['X'] suddenly came through Audrey, very loud and almost aggressive: (singing at the start) "Hallelujah, Hallelujah… Lift up your eyes unto the Heavens. You children will not stop looking through that glass darkly, to see the light that is above. You have so much negative thought within your world that it is stopping the light coming through. You are letting the devas get hold of those negative thoughts and are turning them in on yourselves. You must break this. You must turn those negative thoughts into positive ones. Stop thinking all the time of negativity."

He was then asked about his name. "My name is not important! I have not come here for self-indulgence, but to tell you that the time is near for you to change the attitudes of your natures. Your world is a beautiful colour seen from above. The colour of blue – and what is the colour of blue mean? Answer me!" The words spirituality and peace were offered by the circle. "Healing and spirituality. It is time for you all to realise this. What do you do? You kill yourselves! You kill everything else on your Earth plane.

"You must lift those vibes! You have got to let the changing energies come through. This is a planet of learning, and it is time that the human race graduated. So stop looking within yourselves and sing to the heavens! Hallelujah! Lift those vibes! If you cannot accept this…"

Circle: "Yes we can. Please tell us more."

'X': " You must sweep away all negativity within yourselves. Go out into your world, and help people to see that negativity only kills. There is too much of it. There is an imbalance. It is like the scales – overweight. Will you set this right for me?"

Circle: "We will try. It is not easy in this negative world of ours."

'X': "See, you are being negative now!"

Circle: "We all wish to work, we do what we can, we spread the word."

'X': "Good!"

Circle: "We sow the seed."

'X': "Yes! Yes! Sing the praises on high. Let people know that there is no death."

Circle: "We do. We try. We know that life is eternal."

'X': "That is correct. And what you give, you shall receive. I have now
 completed my lesson."

Circle: "Can you not give us a name?"

'X': "No my friend, no. Names are not important, only the message."

Circle: "Yes, but we would like you to come again, and to know that you are here."

'X': "Well, I will come again, but I cannot say whether I will tell you."

Circle: "Be positive please."

'X': "It is not a case of positivity."

Circle: "We ask in humility. We ask, as it is a human weakness for wanting a name."

'X': "I will consider."

Circle: "We were left a bit speechless by the power of your message."

'X': "Know that every thought that you think goes out like an arrow."

Circle: "It is the hardest part to think correctly, to control the monkey mind."

'X': "Yes, I will come again."

Circle: "We have got the message."

'X': "Make sure that you live up to the message."

Circle: "We will try."

'X': "It is only for your own benefits that I tell you this. For if we were not concerned about the negativity we would not come through. It is like a mother teaching a child. The child does not always listen to the parent. But as the child grows up to beyond the teenage years, he realises that the lessons the parents tried to teach were sensible. So we are trying to teach you. You have gone beyond your teenage years and are coming to maturity. So please don't let the adults within your world to act still like children. We send you all love. May peace be with you."

When Audrey came back she drank a glass of water straight down! I found it surprising that Chi did not come through to say anything, but maybe Audrey was glad to get back! We had a discussion over tea and cake, except for myself. Due to feeling ill I settled for a couple of teaspoonfuls of Bernard's kaolin mixture!

27/07/95 I was absent. [The next circle was cancelled.]

10/08/95 In Arrow Park Hospital, Wirral! Found out that I need my gall bladder removed.

17/08/95 Just Bernard and I. We had a short meditation for about half an hour, and then a chat over tea. [Next circle was cancelled.]

31/08/95 All present again. We had meditation without music; quite long, and I felt several different presences. Eventually Chi came through: " Good evening. It has been a moon past since we have met. I have come this evening to ask if you would help me. I have a young lady here who is extremely upset. I am afraid she is one of the people who had an overdose of drugs.
  "She is a very young girl, she is only seventeen just. She was in full time with her baby. She did not mean to do this. She had a weak heart, and she only took a little – but it was enough. And she is so desperate for her baby to see life on Earth. She feels that she has taken the baby's life away from her, and she wishes that the baby may be allowed to be within your circle when you sit, so she can understand a little of what she should have had – of the life that she should have had when she came down on Earth. I have been trying desperately to quieten the girl down, she is so upset about it." (We sent our love to her, etc.)
  "The baby's name is Geraldine. Her name is Gladys – Gladys Herbert. She just would like the baby to be in the middle of your circle." (We all said that she would be most welcome, and so forth.)
  "Thank you. She is happy at that. Of course, as you yourselves may realise, that this infant will be allowed to physically come back to Earth. But at the moment, to give Gladys peace and comfort, we would be very grateful. She is now calming down a little.
  "I will give you a quick description of Gladys herself. When on Earth she was taller than my lady, but not too tall, with fair hair and a pretty complexion. Her baby should have had a light golden hair with a touch of summer sunshine in it. She should have had green eyes like her mother's. I think, if you could be so kind, as before you start your circle, if it could be possible to have some gentle music for the child. This would please her mother greatly. Is this possible?" (Yes.)
  "I will leave you now, for though you do not know it, my lady has

been working very hard before this." We expressed our thanks and that we would be asking for healing for mother and child.

"Thank you. She will of course receive this. But your accepting of her child will be of great comfort to her. For the guilt she feels is very deep at the moment. Peace be with you. Until we meet again."

7/09/95 All present. Mike stayed awake, as we meditated to 'Tranquility' music. I found it hard as usual, but feel I'm getting to grips with the 'body'! Bernard nearly away, but putting the tape off made him 'jump'! After about forty-five minutes Chi came through: "Good evening. Gladys has been here, with Geraldine of course. She liked the music very much indeed. She was sitting cross-legged with the baby on your floor over there." Chi was asked if she felt more at ease now.

"A little. She tells us that she was very depressed one night. She didn't really mean to take as much as she had. She didn't realise it would have the effect that it did. She was just trying to frighten somebody – her parents. I'm afraid it went a little too far for her. Really she is still in a state of shock you know."

Circle: "If we sent her our thoughts would this help?"
Chi: "Oh yes. It will take a little time of course. She is so full of guilt for all the things that have happened to her. But I am sure that your loving thoughts that you send out to her will help greatly. She will be counselled, but at the moment she is not in that state to understand. She has got to be given time, and this is why she needs this connection, not just for Geraldine, but for herself."
Circle: "She is welcome to come to this circle anytime."
Chi: "Thank you. She was given to me to bring down to this circle, for we know that you understand. We do wish to use you."
Circle: "You wish to use us?"
Chi: "Yes."
Circle: "We are willing."
Chi: "We know you are. We wish to use you, in rescue. It will not always be a rescue, for a rescue circle can be very demanding."
Circle: "We would be very willing to do that, we are very willing to help, we are all committed."

Chi: "They have also got plans for work in a different way for my lady."

Circle: "This is the circle friend, is it? Can you tell us of the plans?"

Chi: "It is just being formulated. I have said enough. I will give you more information in a little while. But suffice to say that your circle has got to work. You see, within your circle, we have gathered here souls that have different experiences of life. You have all learned your lessons. You have all experienced different sorrows, different lessons, different knowledge, and the combination is a good one. You will be able to understand and sympathise, and help the souls that come down. But do not think that we will throw the book at you, as the saying goes, too quickly. We will not throw you in at the deep end. Is that the correct saying?"

Circle: "Yes."

Chi: "Gladys is now singing her baby to sleep. She is content at the moment. Her, her guilt goes out to her mother. We know and understand that you are having problems with your group. We will try and help. I will say goodnight and God bless."

Circle: "Goodnight."

Chi: "Though the willow tree may droop – its roots go deep into the earth and it draws its nourishment from deep down within the earth. May you all be like the willow tree, spread your branches and use them like an umbrella, like the willow tree."

Tea and discussion afterwards.

14/09/95 All present. I put a soft zebra toy in the area that Audrey said where Gladys was last time. Meditation was to 'Africa' tape. Maybe those two things prompted Zimbala to come through after about twenty-five minutes: "Good evening friends."

Circle: "Good evening. Do you like the music?"

Zimbala: "Yes, friends. I have come here tonight to tell you what has been happening to your little friend that you had here with the baby. And that music also brought me. But of course you know that I love children. I have never told you before, but I helped to carve the crèche for the little ones you know. And my wives helped me too! Along with other people of course.

"But she has just been introduced to us, she has now calmed herself enough. We are so pleased with the little toy that you have so kindly brought her. Actually, I like the little toy too! As it reminds me of when I was on the Earth plane. You know, when we used to go hunting, we would wear the skins of the zebras – as you call them – to help us approach the animals. We would also collect the urine and put it over the skin. But to get back to tell you about the little one. She is with you and maybe soon she will talk with you, as she has calmed down a lot. I told her I would come with her tonight. We have so many little ones! You do know my name don't you?"

Circle: "Zimbala. Has it any meaning?"

Zimbala: "Yes, but the meaning now does not mean anything. I am not what I thought I was when I was on your Earth plane."

Circle: "Can I ask if you still help with the healing?"

Zimbala: "I help with the little ones. Your little ones have got older now haven't they?"

Circle: "Yes! I would say so friend."

Zimbala: "I have not been around very often, as there is so much work. You do understand don't you?"

Circle: "Yes."

Zimbala: "If I do not manage to get here for some time, I will keep Chi informed. He is always around you know. Chi and I get on very well together. I think sometimes that he thinks I should be more serious! I will leave you my friends. May the sunrise always be bright for you." After only a short while, Chi came through.

Chi: "Good evening! As you have just been told, our little friend has got over her weeping. She is still very dazed, but is coming to terms. She would very much like her mother to know that she is alright, but we are telling her that at the moment her mother is not in a fit state. She would not be able to accept it at the moment. There is a lot of anger mixed up with the severe loss. But with patience, perhaps one day, we will see what we can do."

Circle: "We are willing to help."

Chi: "Yes we know. It may be possible at some time to be able to pass a message on to another medium who may be able to be near. But at the moment the mother would not even think of going. Of course, the child is missing her mother – and her father. There was a very loving relationship between the father and the daughter. She is just telling me that she used to love the song, 'The Little Red Rooster'."

Circle: "The Rolling Stones – we will play it next week."

Chi: "That would be very nice."

Circle: "I'm not sure if it's to your taste!"

Chi: "Well it is for her." Mike then went on to ask a question about the 'Reverend' [Hallelujah!] who came through several weeks ago.

Chi: "You are quite right. Yes, we do know of this gentleman. I'm afraid he is beginning to annoy quite a lot of people in your world. He is making his mark, and he is very forceful, as you will have observed. He was a lay preacher and he came from America, and he was taken suddenly. In the middle of a meeting he had a heart attack I believe, in the middle of one of his sermons! I'm afraid I have to laugh – he is still giving his sermons."

Circle: "He has not been rescued then, my friend?"

Chi: "Well, he is quite happy as he is at the moment. He does not really need rescued, he is as he is, he will gradually calm down."

Bernard: "May I ask a question?"

Chi: "It is question time tonight!"

Bernard: "Any news of my lady?"

Chi: "Your lady is, yes… actually, I was enquiring about her last week and she is very well. She is working very hard, but she is enjoying herself."

Bernard: "I have not heard her speak to me yet."

Chi: "You must not worry too much about this you know. The fact that she is with us must be enough. Of course, you did know that she loved flowers and gardening. [Yes.] She is learning all about different plants that she did not come across before. She is being taught how to propagate these plants, so she will be able to pass information down to people. Eventually, down onto your Earth plane, because you will desperately need this information and this will be her job. She has got all kinds of books around her.

"They are telling me that in her spare time she is building a beautiful chapel out of flowers. There is a group of them, all ladies. They are telling me that there are six of them. It is just a happy pastime for them. How is Joyce?"

Bernard: "Joy?"
Chi: "Yes."
Bernard: "Joy has to see a specialist in November about her head. My good lady and Joy were very close."
Chi: "She is telling me that she will be there."
Bernard: "Thank you."
Chi: "Did she like to – she is giving me the name of Arthur Daley, and that she liked to watch Arthur Daley."
Bernard: "Minder, on TV – yes! She did."
Chi: "She said she liked his scheming."
Bernard: "My good lady was a bit of a schemer herself."
Chi: "That is why she liked him then!"
Bernard: "In the kindest possible way."
Chi: "And she is also giving me the name Alfred. Do you remember the name Alfred she is saying?"
Bernard: "No. I have difficulty in remembering sometimes."
Chi: "She said he had something to do with the roads."
Bernard: "No, no."
Chi: "She is calling you a silly old toffer!"
Bernard: "She quite often called me that!"
Chi: "And she is having a good laugh at you, but she also gives you a good hug."
Bernard: "I love her very much."
Chi: "Yes, she knows. She is saying, please do not weep for me, for you still have much work to do down here."
Bernard: "Thank you very much."

Chi: "And you must keep your emotions for those that need it here."

Bernard: "That I will do. I am pleased to be able to work."

Chi: "I don't know why but I'm getting 'Jingle Bells'. Do you understand that?"

Bernard: "Yes. Christmas is not so very far away, and she loved Christmas."

Chi: "She is telling me that you must put some holly over the doorway here."

Bernard: "Yes. I understand."

Chi: "We are waiting for you all to gather your forces, with patience. You will become strong. We have this other person who will enter your circle."

Circle: "Do we know them?"

Chi: "Yes, you do! But we have to have patience. When this other person is available to enter, it will be like the last link in the circle, and you will become very strong. Then it will be time for you to work."

Circle: "We will look forward to that."

Chi: "At the moment you do! We have got to be patient – on both sides. There is much work to be done. You do know … You must accept things that are extremely hard for humans to accept. Over so many centuries you have tied yourselves up in knots. It is extremely hard for you to let go of the things that you have been taught – and it is not just over this one lifetime. Especially for you people in the West. The old barriers have got to be broken before it is too late.

"It is coming. There are so many spirit friends that are trying to help. I was listening to you this afternoon – it is a very good idea about what you said – about the tree!"

Circle: "The tree my friend?"

Chi: "Yes! Have you forgotten already? What did I give you last week?

Circle: "Oh yes! The symbol of the willow tree."

Chi: "That is right! You will all need your roots to go very deep, for this work is very important. Please do not forget that we are here to help you."

Circle: "We are willing."

Chi: "We will seize on any soul that is willing! I will now say goodnight. And if you see that symbol you will know that I am with you. May the light go with you, surround you, protect you, and give you strength."

21/09/95 All present. We had no introduction! Put on a Rolling Stones tape that included 'Little Red Rooster'. Found it difficult to clear the mind – was listening and joining in singing the songs in my head! Also had a few pains, especially my jaw. Thought Audrey would give a voice a few times, but it wasn't until an hour later that Chi finally came through: "Good evening friends. I have been here for some time. But I don't know if you have realised, but you have been very privileged to have someone here who has come from afar. And I myself feel very humble.

"As for the music, I must say that it is not mine! But Gladys liked it! She showed me what she used to do, and it has cheered her up no end. She used to put her head down and bring her arms up, like two wings, and flap them and make a noise, and her little doggie would yowl along with her. And it used to make her very happy – and it made her happy tonight. But we all have had quite an experience."

Circle: "May we know who came?"

Chi: "I am not at liberty to say. Only that they are very wise and very powerful."

Circle: "There were more than one then my friend?"

Chi: "Well, there were a few, but there was one in particular."

Circle: "Is there a reason for this?"

Chi: "I believe that you will be told sometime, yes. But they are so powerful, that it is going to take quite a time for us all to get used to the energies that are being brought down. I must confess that I do not know the exact reason, for it took me by surprise as well."

Circle: "You were a long time deliberating tonight my friend."

Chi: "Well, do you not realise that I could not come through?

Circle: "Were you able to communicate with them?"

Chi: "I was made to feel very humble. They did not deliberately do so. But they come from a different level. A much higher level than I have achieved. If they come again I feel that it will take some time to accept the power. The energy of my lady will have to be raised, and they will have to bring down theirs to an acceptable level."

Circle: "How can we raise the energy of my lady?"

Chi: "We will see. We will work very close to her. This information, I feel, must not be broadcast at the moment."

Circle: "We will be guided by you."

Chi: "We will all need patience. I thank you once again on behalf of our little one for the music, it has cheered her up no end. I will leave now."

Circle: "Will we play the same music next time?"

Chi: "I think that may be enough! Well *I* feel it may be enough, though I don't know if she will accept that!"

Circle: "Perhaps we will just put on 'Little Red Rooster' for her."

Chi: "That may be a very good idea!"

When Audrey came back she was feeling really sick. She said she had never experienced anything like it before. She reported that she saw a really bright light, but golden rather than white. She had pains down her right side and her stomach had felt totally 'empty'. Bernard remarked that he had pains in his arms and had had a vision: a bright bowl, like cut glass, but in silver, had come towards him and a voice said, "You may also taste" or words to that effect.

Regrettably I seem to be the insensitive one, as I had felt little and had no inkling of the presence. Tea and cake.

28/09/95 All present. We played 'Little Red Rooster' first and then another tape was put on. I felt lots of energy and the presence of spirit. We stopped after nearly an hour. Audrey then told us that she had been told that nothing would come through for a while, and she had been given breathing exercises to do. There was a good discussion over tea, about the willow design for T-shirts or badges. Then Mike and Audrey asked about 'C' coming into the circle. I said I thought it a bit too soon; she has only just started on the path. I feel Audrey is forcing the pace too much. Bernard very anti at present, and agreed that she needs some control before joining our circle. Spirit will guide.

5/10/95 All present. 'Little Red Rooster' put on before the circle had convened! Then meditation to the 'sea waves' tape. I actually got totally relaxed in body *and* mind, for an instant, but at least it happened. Nobody came through, but Audrey reported that 'they' were building bricks of light, and had got three layers done. She also got what she called hieroglyphics, but I couldn't make them out at all. Tea and biscuits.

12/10/95 All present. Mike forgot to bring his tapes, as did I. So all we had was 'Little Red Rooster' and then meditated in silence. I found it difficult as usual, but felt some presence – even felt 'something' brush my right leg. I came out of it after half an hour, and Audrey followed a little later. However, the other two lasted for about an hour. Tea and cake after closing the meeting.

19/10/95 All present. Bernard a bit down, as his in-laws are moving away to Wales soon, and he is feeling very much on his own. Usual start, 'Little Red Rooster' and then meditation to 'Africa' tape. Getting a bit better at relaxing. Very heavy breathing from Audrey, but no voice for quite some time. I felt a big surge of energy just before she spoke. The voice was a new one, no name, and spoke with lots of long pauses – energy must have been low. I missed the first part but this is roughly what was said after Mike asked if our energies were low: "The light within you, the light of the world is within your being. You hide this light with doubt, and things that have to be… when we give you signs there is doubt. When things happen there is doubt. You must release yourselves from the doubt and know that we are here.

"Trust and believe the things that you are given. You must expand your energies." (In which way friend?) "You must not doubt in the things that we give as signs, for we cannot reach within you if you do not expand your energies. We are waiting. We are waiting to work. You do not understand?" (No not really, could you tell us what we are doing wrong?) "What I will say is that you are not giving of yourselves. You are not trusting also in the signs that you are given."

(Which is the connection with these signs?) "You must lay aside the doubts that you have within your circle. Love and trust.

"The universe can be open unto you. Oh children, we love you so much." (We love you too. Is this your first visit to us?) "No." (Have you spoken before to us?) "No." (We must be more positive within the circle?) "That is what is needed. Do not forget that you are the light of the world, all that believe in us. We need your lights to lift the shutters completely." (Thank you for your words.) "There is what you would call an army of us waiting to enter your doors. I will leave you all now." (Thank you.) "Do not forget! Though there are clouds in the sky, the sun is always there."

The meeting was closed and then tea. We discussed 'C' again and Bernard's problems.

26/10/95 All present. Bernard with an abscess on his right jaw – having to take antibiotics as he had collapsed a few days earlier with the poison going round his system. Played 'Little Red Rooster', but Mike couldn't get his tape to work, so we meditated in silence – which I felt was quite a good idea. Lots of 'feelings', seemed to be presences, and it went better than usual.

After a while Audrey went into some deep breathing, but then stopped. Just when I thought nothing was going to happen, Chi came through.

"Good evening. I will only stay a short while. Gladys and Geraldine are doing very well now. She thanks you for the 'Little Red Rooster'. She loves it and it has settled her greatly. I won't stay long. If things do not happen – or you think they do not happen from week to week – do not get despondent, for they are definitely happening. Things are building up, and they have asked me to thank you all for being so constant each week. They know that you believe and trust in us. There have been many here tonight. I must go now for my lady's sake."

Audrey came out feeling quite sick, but recovered after five or ten minutes. She said she felt her head expanding! We had tea and a chat.

2/11/95 All present. Played 'Little Red Rooster', and then as last week meditated in silence. I didn't do so well this week, but felt a few of the energies. I couldn't stop the thoughts, and was on the point of giving up when Chi came through.

"Good evening friends. Again I will not be staying long. I have been given to give to you this Bowl of Light. It is placed in the middle of your circle and this Light is all that you will need to feed on. It is like the bee with the nectar. It will be your nourishment. Think upon this Light, this

Bowl within your circle, and take what you need from it. You may draw it up within your breath or wash your hands in it. It is there for you to use, to gather enlightenment and strength.

"Before I go, I must apologise for last time that we met. I was very lax in not appreciating what you have done. The work that you have put in with the badges – I think that they are rather beautiful. Do not just wear them as a symbol, but be like the tree. Think also upon it as your stabaliser, and gather all within its branches. I thank you once again.

"You will find, friends, that if you drink from the Bowl of Light, soon you will gather more and more. More and more souls will be drawn to you for knowledge, for your world is crying out for it. If at times you feel lost in an answer that you must give – think upon that Bowl, and be like the tree, and you will not go wrong. We all send our love to you. And your efforts are much appreciated. We are now gathering our strength. I will say goodnight. We will meet again soon." Tea and biscuits.

9/11/95 All present. Played 'Little Red Rooster' and then into meditation without music. Usual for me, but I did feel a few 'energies' around. After about an hour, Audrey did her deep breathing, and then a voice came through that we hadn't heard before – in a sort of drawn out whisper: "I've been preparing the body. I've been making the body more supple. I will be with you soon. Peace be with you all. You will see me and know me soon by my lights. Go walk in your true lights."

Audrey said that she saw three rings at the start, not set quite vertical; then a lighted candle in a pyramid, and thirdly three stars. That sounded as if it could be somehow connected to Orion, and the Ancient Egyptians. Tea and cake. Mike and Audrey away next week.

16/11/95 Just Bernard and myself. Played 'Little Red Rooster' and meditated in silence for about an hour. Felt presences, but Bernard got some flowers and autumn leaves – probably sent to him by his wife. Had tea and biscuits and a long discussion about the path we are on, etc. Bernard still not sure about staying where he is. Quite a frost, with clear skies – saw a shooting star when I came out to the car, and a deer just before the mill.
23/11/95 All present, though Mike and Audrey delayed. So they missed 'Little Red Rooster'. We meditated to 'Summer Garden' tape. I had my

usual difficulty, not helped by a sore throat and a bit of a cold, and was often heading towards sleep! Nothing from anyone tonight. Audrey felt 'work' on her solar plexus area, and got an image of a chair with material like velvet, richly embroidered with a heart shape. Also the words 'Prince Rennock of Cleeves' came into the story somehow. Tea and cake and then home for a hot drink and bed.

30/11/95 Audrey still recovering from 'flu like symptoms, so only three of us present. After 'Little Red Rooster' we meditated to 'Ocean Waves'. Felt the presence of spirit, especially when I was grounding myself as the 'willow'. However, never got very deep because my gall bladder has been playing up for several days now, though feel that the music is quite good to 'switch off' to. I did sense a 'person' moving around us. After an hour we stopped and had Elderflower cordial and sparkling water to celebrate the end of my first year with the circle!

7/12/95 All present. Played 'Little Red Rooster' and then meditated in silence. As last time, when grounding as the willow tree, I felt it done with power and it seemed easy to do. I was a bit more relaxed this week. After about thirty minutes Chi came through: "Good evening friends. Our faithful friends! We have been very pleased the way you sit and meet. Of course, we do understand when there are times when it is not possible for you to meet. We are not as inflexible as you people think we are.

"I would like to say as we are now coming to the end of your year, I would like to tell you how some of our friends are getting on. Gladys is doing extremely well. She has realised she can do more in spirit than she could do on the Earth plane. Her baby is very beautiful, and she is losing that sadness about her, in fact, she is really a very bright spirit.

"And Joe! Now Joe is going to be reborn. He is going to be one of twins. He has met up with another spirit who was on the Earth plane and led a similar type of life as himself. They have come very close and they will be reborn into your world in the new year. Let me say, I think that the mother might have a lot of trouble from them both! But she will be very happy with this. They will be what you call a 'bundle of mischiefs'! But they are both very good spirits. They will be reborn in the same country as last time, but in a place called Durham. I have been told that the mother's name is Joyce.

"Sister Anna is often with my lady, though she does not realise it, she is around. She is also doing a great deal of work for the spirit world.

"Your lady is doing extremely well with her agriculture. Of course she sends you all her love. [Bernard: "Thank you, and I send mine'.] She wants to tell you that she will be going to a dance, and that she's got a rather lovely gold dress for the occasion. [Bernard: "Lovely."]

"You may not know, but this year has been terribly productive on your side, but I can assure you that things are going as they should. Enjoy yourselves over your period – of Yuletide."

Mike then asked if he could put a question, and with a 'yes' from Chi, he enquired about the 'reverend'.

"I believe you have asked this question before! As I previously said, he was of a religious bent on your Earth plane. He came from America. He was a coloured gentleman. We are now teaching him that he cannot go around frightening people who are so willing to help us! That the way to go about it is not the way that he did it. He is so concerned about your world, that he felt that the only way he could get the message over, is demonstrating as he did. But he is now learning that there are other ways, and that you do not have to be a 'bull in a china shop'! Does that answer your question? ["Yes".]

"I would like to tell you about how the spirit enters the new born, and when it enters. I know that there is an awful lot of confusion. The spirit will enter the foetus at about the time of 40 of your weeks, but it is kept to a very low key, and it is not developed fully until the baby is born into your world. As you may say, it is asleep. It has to come down, as you know, through the different layers. This takes energy, so spirit has to rest within the foetus. Then as the child comes into the world, as it takes its first breath, so the spirit awakes within the child. I hope this will end a lot of confusion about the question. [Bernard queried 40 weeks, as gestation was about 36.]

"Now you see is that ... you do not realise that the spirit knows before! Also that the nine months – it is nearer ten.

"Will you please tell my lady that there is a Reginald Hammond here?
Mike: "Yes, how is he?"
Chi: "He has progressed greatly. He is laughing, he is saying he can remember the ear twisting.

Mike: "Your lady will find this very amusing. He had an enormous shock."

Chi: "Yes. He was very concerned about his child. But he has now grown up into a very decent young man. And he has had a lot of help from his family. Anthony has given him an awful lot of help. He is saying that he was extremely angry."

Mike: "He is happier now then?"

Chi: "He came to terms with it a long time ago now. But when he first passed the anger was great within him."

Mike: "Is he helping in spirit?"

Chi: "Yes. He has done an awful lot of studying. I think he said that he was not very good at it on the Earth plane. He is telling me … he is saying that Sid has not had a very happy life. That he was a very sensitive man and that his life was not as it should have been. Is there anything that you would like to ask?"

Me: "Is there anything more we can do to develop ourselves, that we are not already doing?"

Chi: "No. All I would say is just to meditate and it will come. It is very difficult, we realise, for a lot of you to get through that barrier. It is not your fault, for you have been 'barred' up for so many generations with what you have been told by your religious sects, and through your childhood at home and at school. It is very difficult to completely take the curtain down and see. Do not try too hard. As I think you have been told it is a matter of letting go.

"If you like to think of it as rather like the surface of a pond. That you are in the water under the surface. The pond has got a coating that is hard to break through, something like you might have – a sticky substance on the top, that you have to break through this to the air beyond. But once you have done this you will never go back again. You will find it getting easier and easier.

"Do not put aside things that you think are just your imagination. And if you go to give to somebody and you think it is just my imagination, I feel silly for doing this in case it is wrong, it does not matter. It shows us that you are trying and opening up, and the more you give, the better you will become at it. Don't be frightened of making yourself look silly, for that is only the ego. I think that you will find that as you progress in the coming months, things will progress for you all.

"I have a young boy here. He was spastic. He has been here listening for some time now. He says he wishes to sit within your circle from now on. ["He's welcome."] His name is John. At the moment he is coming down as he was, but as he gets more accustomed and he realises that he doesn't have to show himself as he was on the Earth plane, he will be able to move better and speak to you. He is laughing. He is so pleased that you will accept him. He thinks he has to come in his wheelchair."

Circle: "We will make a space for him. There's plenty of room by the fire."
Chi: "He is laughing freely now! I must go."
Mike: "Your lady hasn't been too well lately."
Chi: "No. Have to build her up again. Have a nice holiday. I think you will have a very busy one."
Mike: "Yes."
Chi: "Take care. Do not let any accidents happen. 'The bells are ringing for me and my girl', I believe that you will understand this?"
Bernard: "Yes! Will you tell her to have a good time at the dance!"
Chi: "She is being very cheeky at the moment!"
Bernard: "What is she saying?"
Chi: "That she is going to dance with your father."
Bernard: "They should get along very well together."
Chi: "She is nodding. God bless you all."
Tea and cake.

14/12/95 All present. Started with 'Little Red Rooster' and then silent meditation. After forty minutes Audrey started her heavy breathing, and then a voice came. But it was so soft and indistinct that it was difficult to hear. The spirit was obviously finding it difficult to come through. Much of the voice was lost in long drawn-out words: "I am Khan. I am Kahoon."

Circle: "Kaloon? Kham?"
K: "Kaahlo....."
Circle: "Kalhoon, yes friend."
K: "Kaahlune."

Circle: "We welcome you friend to our circle."
K: "I am finding it very difficult."
Mike interrupted: "Difficult, yes friend. Is your instrument struggling friend?"
K: "No!"
Mike: "Have you had difficulty in reaching this level?"
K: "Yeeeesssssssssss. I have tried before."
Mike: "Yes, we have had some indication, you have succeeded this time friend."
K: "I was the manservant of Ramess the second."
Mike: "Thank you friend."
K: "I was called Raaa…."
Mike: "Called who friend? Ra?"
K: "My name was Khahoom."
Mike: "And you were manservant to Ramesses the second, the great warrior Pharaoh?"
K: "Yes."
Mike: "And your purpose in visiting us?"
K: " This you will learn in the future. It is sufficient that I have managed so far. I walked in the shadow of my master."
Mike: "Some shadow."
He left then, and we had tea and biscuits.

11/01/96 All present. Played 'Little Red Rooster' and meditated in silence. After about forty-five minutes I heard Audrey starting to breathe deeply, but it didn't last long. Very near the end I felt elated, so knew there was a powerful presence near. We stopped at the hour mark and closed the circle. Audrey said that Khahoom had been there, and that she had seen lots of crystals and lights. She felt that he was building up to something. I thought that would indeed be very interesting. Then tea and cake.

18/01/96 Bernard ill, so meeting cancelled.

25/01/96 All present. Played 'Little Red Rooster' and meditated to 'Pharaoh' tape. Not very successful, and not just me this time. Partly due maybe by the coldness of the room. Closed before the hour and had tea and cake.

1/02/96 All present. Played 'Little Red Rooster' and meditated in silence. I concentrated on my breathing to try and get properly relaxed. Started of by counting my breathing – 3 breaths to the minute and then relaxed that to 4 or 5, and eventually just about 'let go'. After about an hour Chi came through: "Good evening friends. I will not be long in staying, but I would just like to say that you must not feel that it is a waste of time sitting here. Things are happening. Patience on your part!

"I would rather like you all to do an experiment for me, when you are sitting by yourselves meditating. Will, when you close your eyes, take your inner eye, and send it round the insides of your heads, going from left to right. Go round and round the insides of your head and see what happens. Fasten it up, getting faster and faster. Will you do this for me? (Replies: "Certainly, sure.") And I will ask you next time when we meet how you felt – what happens.

"I would just like to say a very quick word of what my lady says to herself – well, not always to herself! As she does not always say it every day – she forgets sometimes, but I think it is rather nice, and very ... She says – and I will speak for her – you are part of everything that ever was, that ever is, and that ever shall be. We *are* a part of everything that ever was. There is no beginning and no end – it is eternal. So the beginning is now and the future is now. Can you understand that? (Yes/certainly/ and silence!)

"And also that you are a part of the Earth, are made up from the Earth, the iron that is within the Earth, the crystals that are within the Earth, everything that the Earth holds. You are made of the water. Without the water in your bodies, your Earthly beings, you would be shriveled up, no bigger than the size of an almond. So you are part of the water.

"You are part of the air, for without that air you would not exist. You are a part of fire, for without that energy, again you would not exist. And do honour the oneness of all that is. For you *are* that oneness. And everything that is in the universe is in with you.

"But please remember to do that experiment for me – will you? It will be interesting to know the results. You do know that you have had a higher entity with you this evening? (Yes) They are both finding it rather difficult.

Mike: "Is that on their part?"

Chi: "Both my lady's part and .."

Mike: "Theirs? My lady is not relaxed enough?"

Chi: "It is not that. It is not that. It is different you see, the energies are different. It will take time."

Circle: "Any news of our friends from the past – little Joe?"

Chi: "Yes, he is now back on your Earth plane. He and his twin brother."

Mike: "He was born on Arran, the Isle of Arran."

Chi: "Were they now!"

Mike: "That is what you said before."

Chi: "No, no, no."

Mike: "I must have misunderstood you."

Me: "Durham I think."

Chi: "That is correct."

Mike: "With age comes hard of hearing – may I ask you to forgive me."

Chi: "I will forgive you! There is nothing to forgive. Yes, they will both be very lively babies. One will support the other. They are going to be extremely close – they *are* extremely close – as they grow up. They will fight for each other's rights. I will keep you informed of how they are getting on."

Mike: "Thank you."

Chi: "Their surname is Harrington. It is David and John. Sister Anna also is doing very well. She is happy, helping the children, seeing to the sick."

Circle: "What of Gladys?"

Chi: "Gladys is beginning to realise that she wants to work. She has been taken into tender loving care – her and her little one. She is not quite sure what she wants to do yet. One second she wants to do one thing and then another. But she will settle down to one thing and she will ... we are hoping that she might teach, but of course this is up to her. She has a very lively mind, and she is good with the little ones. But we will have to wait for her own decision. Really at the moment she is too interested in seeing all the places for her to settle on one thing. We will give her time.

"Now I think I must leave you. I will say a thing before I go .."

Bernard interrupted with: "Is there any news of my lady?"

Chi: "May I leave that until next time?"

Bernard: "Yes."

Chi: "As I was just going to say quickly, thank you for wearing your badges!"

We then closed and had tea and cake.

8/02/96 Meeting cancelled due to snow.

15/02/96 All present. Played 'Little Red Rooster' and then went into the silence. Felt a presence after twenty minutes or so. Had difficulty with stomach and intestines gurgling away. After an hour had passed, sensed Bernard had his sore leg, and sure enough Chi came through: "Good evening friends. We will not be long tonight. Things have been happening, and one has been with my lady who has needed to be with her. [Audrey later said she felt her mother there.]

"I have come to tell you about Gladys and I think you wished to know. She has been assigned the job of taking care of the little ones. She is now over her grief and she is well on the way to recovery. She is a merry soul and she makes the little ones laugh. She is so grateful for you playing the 'Little Red Rooster'. For she does this dance to the little ones when she hears that. And they laugh so merrily! It is beautiful to see.

"I will say that you must have patience. You understand this? (Yes) Things will come together." Somebody then asked if John was here tonight. Chi replied: "John came along a little while ago. He was a very poor soul on your Earth plane, and it is very difficult for him to realise that he does not have to carry this burden he had on your Earth plane. But the more you can think of him and send your loving thoughts, the more the energy will increase the wellbeing of his spiritual soul.

'My dear friend, you often wonder why your loved one does not get in contact with you? Is this so?" Bernard agreed. "Well, she is around you. But you must realise that her condition was a very hard one. And we would not have her come back to this Earth plane with that condition. Can you understand this?"

Bernard: "Yes. I would not wish her to."

Chi: "It is difficult you know, to come back through the heaviness of your material world and not realise that you do not have to carry this burden of the material, as you come back down. It is a lesson that we have to learn when we become guides, and when we wish to get in contact with you on this plane. But, she receives the messages through the ethers, as we all do. And of course you know that she is with you – don't you?"

Bernard: "Yes, I do."

Chi: "It is very easy for us over here, and also for you people on Earth, to say, "Do not be lonely." We understand. When you love a soul and you materially lose the sight of that person, that you think that they are not with you. But they are only in the next room. There is only a very thin door between your world and the one that the souls go to, to start with. I hope this does not make you feel even sadder!"

Bernard: "No, no. You have explained it very well. I would not wish her to suffer in any way."

Chi: "It is very understandable. She knows – as you in your heart know – that you will meet again. I will say goodnight. And if in the weeks to come you feel that there is not a lot going on within your circle, do not get despondent, for a lot is happening."

Bernard: "Thank you."

Chi: "Do be like your tree! Give love to all that you meet. Even if it is difficult at times! You know, plants will not grow without nourishment. So you must be as the nourishment and feed the poor souls, feed their roots, as the tree feeds through its roots, and becomes a magnificent sight to see. God bless you all."

Then tea and cake. We agreed to start half an hour later next week, due to a work commitment of mine. In the car on the way home, felt a presence with me – 'touched' my left hand and my face.

22/02/96 All present. Played 'Little Red Rooster' and meditated in silence. Usual problems, tried to visualise the Bowl of Light, but just couldn't do it. Chi came through: "Good evening friends. I have been observing…people…and I was wondering why it is that you act as if you are in a maze. You get yourself into a maze and you come to *so* many dead ends. You get yourself so confused over issues that you go round and round. May I say that rats get put in boxes as experiments, you human beings do the same thing. You go up this alley and it is a dead end, so you go a different way and that is also a dead end. And when you do eventually get to the middle – you think you are so clever! But then you lose your way again trying to get back out! [Circle then asked what did he recommend, etc.]

"You need to <u>see</u>, and I appreciate that it is not easy for you, that things should go in a straight line. Your thoughts should not dart from one side to another. Negative, negative, negative, so negative. You bump into each other, you go round and round and round. Instead of making for the centre of the point that you are trying to get at. If only man would learn not to keep confusing himself over silly things and arguing with the next person, when all they want is to get to the central point.

"We observe you all, and we would like to help you, but we have to let you find your own way. We try very hard to open peoples' eyes, to open their minds, but we are only allowed to show you. As you know, you have got free wills. And if you don't want to go along that path there is nothing we can do about it. But it is so sad to see you go around and around and around and getting nowhere. There! I have had my lecture!"

Circle: "People are becoming more aware."

Chi: "Yes, yes, yes. But even so you know … I will say no more. Yes, there is a growing movement. Yes there is. I am sorry, I am feeling rather …"

Circle: "Negative?"

Chi: "Well, that is what you would call it. Yes. I am just … I would like to push you along."

Circle: "Is there anyone particular here that needs pushing along?"

Chi: "I will not answer that! You have got to search your own minds."

Circle: "We do try."

Chi: "Yes, we know you do, we know you do. It is just … we look on the world as a whole you know."

Circle: "Not a very happy place."

Chi: "Yes. I think you have been told there are different energies coming into your world, that we would like you all at this time to open up your minds so that you can take in these higher energies. There again, I must not be too impatient must I."

Circle: "I wish you would go on. We always need a bit of prodding now and again."

Chi: "I will save that for another day. Yes."

Circle: "Any more news of the higher entities?"

Chi: "The trouble is, you see, my lady finds it very difficult to believe that she can do it."

Circle: "She can do it of course."

Chi: "Yes. These energies are so much higher than I am. (pause) What do you think my name is?"

Circle: "Chi?"

Chi: "Yes, I will set you that question."

Mike: "Life force."

Chi: "And yourselves?"

Bernard: "Singing bird."

Chi: "Oh, I like that one."

Me: "I thought I read it recently, but I've forgotten!"

Chi: "You've forgotten. Well you see it has two meanings. You are correct in saying it is energy, life force. But it also means service."

Circle: "Which we all must do."

Chi: "Yes, in your different ways. Chi is energy and as I say service. I thought I would just put that one in! Yes, you see, the higher the spiritual energies that wish to come down do find it difficult, and your lady feels she is not capable."

Circle: "What can we do?"

Chi: "Patience, it will come. See, coming down through the different layers of heavier and heavier vibrations, takes a lot of energy for them to do this. It makes them heavy, as you can appreciate. And it is very wearing on them. As they pick up .."

Mike interrupted: "The heavier energies."

Chi: "The heavier energies, yes. So when they first manage to do so it is only for short periods of time, until they, and whoever it is that they use as their instrument, get accustomed. Do you think in the weeks to come you can provide yourself with pads, and coloured pencils, or whatever you have? ("Yes") I think that this will be a very good idea for you all.'

Circle: "A good exercise friend?"

Chi: "Yes. I'm picking up a lot of sickness – illness."

Circle: "Anything specific friend?"

Chi: "Heaviness of the chest. Do you know of anyone who has a chest condition?"

Mike: "Your lady and myself are channeling healing to a lady who is terminally ill, and she has a chest problem."

Chi: "I will say no more. I will say goodnight. As you say – in love and light. Spread your lights. We will see you again. Gladys and John send their love to you."

The circle was closed and we had a long discussion over tea and cake.

29/02/96 All present. Played 'Little Red Rooster' and then silent meditation. After only a short time Chi came through: "Good evening. I see that you brought your pads and your colours. This is very good, I am pleased about this. Because I wish that you will use these pads to open up your emotional minds – not your mental, logical minds but your emotional being. I do not wish you to write, but to put on paper the things that you feel within the circle here. The things that may come to you – perhaps it is a cold draught. Think how you would describe that around whatever area of your body that you feel it. And what colour you would put in. Also it may be heat. Pictures that may be shown to you. I wish you to draw them and not write them, so you will gradually open up your potential for seeing things.

"For I feel that you are very closed and by just using your logical mind and writing things does not help open up that emotional side, as it does when you have to do it in picture form. Do you understand? ("Yes.)

"You are letting more of your emotions go, your imaginations go. So whatever it is that you have felt or you have been sitting here meditating – I will be very interested to see what you have placed on that paper. It is not a competition! It is just learning to let go. For you have been told in the past all you have to do is sit and let go. But we know now that it is very hard for you to do this, so we are giving you this exercise."

Circle: "When do we actually do this? Now?"

Chi: "You can either do it now or when the circle has finished. That is entirely up to you. If you would like to meditate just a little longer, and then close the circle. John, by the way, is very interested in this. Because while he was on your Earth plane he would have very much loved to have drawn, but found it too difficult. His hands would not oblige his mind. But now he is going to school and he is thoroughly enjoying his art lessons. And he is sitting here wondering what you will all do!

"Feel free with colours won't you. I will just give you a very small example. If you have a tickling somewhere on your body, how do you think you would describe that tickling?"

Circle: "With difficulty!"

Chi: "Oh! You do need opening up, don't you!"

Circle: "He is not the only one! We will try – seriously, we will try."

Chi: "I will leave you now and we will see what will happen. Do go with love into light."

Circle: "God bless."

Chi: "God bless you all."

We then went into meditation for ten to fifteen minutes, until suddenly and explosively, Zimbala burst in laughing!

Zimbala: "Ha! Ha! Ha! He has you all there doesn't he! I have been watching him. He is a crafty one that Chi! He is crafty! Oh he is a funny man! I just had to come. He made me laugh so much the way he has got you all! How do you think you would describe a tickle then!

Circle: "I was wondering the same thing friend."

Zimbala: "Don't you know? If I take one of my feathers how would you feel if I tickled you with it?"

Circle: "I think you have supplied the answer then."

Zimbala: "Yes."

Circle: "Have you many feathers in your headdress?"

Zimbala: "Oh yes! Oh yes! Very many."

Circle: "I take it that they would be ostrich feathers friend?"

Zimbala: "Yes. My cloak had feathers too, it was made of feathers. But of course I did not wear that all the time. But that is going back."

Circle: "That was your ceremonial cloak?"
Zimbala: "Mmmm. But now the only feathers I have are the ones that I tickle the babies with! They giggle and laugh. This of course is one way of taking the very sad babies and putting joy within their spirit. There is always method in my madness! Even I can get very upset sometimes, though I do not show them of course, how some of them come into our world. But they are soon happy and gay! Anyway, I must go and let you get on with your task that he has set you! I think I'd get one over on him!"
Circle: "Does he know you are here friend?"
Zimbala: "Yes. We always play these jokes on one another, him and I. He will not tell you this, but he does teach the children all kinds of things. He is very good with his brushwork. Well, bye, bye, for now."
Circle: "Goodbye."
Zimbala: "God bless. May the sun rise on your horizons."

We closed the circle shortly after that and did our 'pictures' before having tea and a chat.

7/03/96 All present. Opened with 'Little Red Rooster' and then into meditation. This was poor for me, pains in my back and just could not settle properly. I grounded well again, and felt one or two 'touches' of energy. After an hour everybody came round and we closed. Tea and biscuits after doing our art exercise.

14/03/96 I was absent due to illness, but lent a tape of what Chi said. "Good evening. I have just come to say, to let you know what is on all your minds. [Dunblane] Our helpers of course are there. We are having a little trouble with the little ones, for some of them of course, are still calling for their mummies, and some have been told by their Earthly parents not to go with strangers. So they are having a little bit of a problem. But you can rest assured that our helpers, like Sister Anna, and our other helpers, will take them all up into their love and care. Of course our friend Zimbala is also there, waiting to gather the little ones to him. As you must realise, these little ones are not the only ones that have to walk into our world.

"We are sending down as much love and healing to all concerned, and the energies that are coming from you all are so wonderful. The colours that we are receiving are very wonderful to see. And in a way, it makes us very happy to realise that there is so much care and love among our spirit friends on Earth. It must be continued to be sent out to <u>all</u> the people concerned, so it acts like a cushion to gently soothe away the deepest and sharpest of their grief.

"It is so very easy to forget after the first shock of these things happening, to forget the people that it has happened to. But if you can remember to give them, for they will need time and support and loving thoughts to be sent to them. It will be very hard as it is, always very hard for people have suffered greatly. For people do not know, do not understand that the spirit continues. They can become very bitter, and this does not do their own advancement any good at all. But we understand. For the more thoughts of love and understanding that are sent out, not just for a week or a month, but for a long time. Will you be able to continue to do this? ("Yes.")

"And you can rest assured that the little ones will come to us. You see, when they are of that age they are still reliant on their parents for their spiritual energies, their own auras are not developed to that extent, and they take from both their parents, or from whoever of the opposite sex that they meet, until their own auras are sufficiently strong. Which in your terms are seven years.

"And they are still trying to be with their own parents. But we have a lot of spiritual children here who will 'entice' them along. We have a few already. But please do not be worried on their behalf. For the love that we have for these children will wrap them. They will be cradled in a house, and Zimbala, and Gladys, and sister Anna, and all the rest, will take them and play with them, and they will love them.

"Of course, you must realise they are not the only helpers we have, there are many of us. Many, many of us. Including somebody else, who at this moment is feeling … we must think about that another time, yes. Yes, I have been told that I can. My lady – you know of my lady?"

Bernard: "Yes."

Chi: "I think I told you she was making in her spare time, a house of flowers, with friends. Well, this house of flowers has been and will be used for children, like the little ones, to play in and around. It is set in the most beautiful garden, with beautiful trees and a most gorgeous setting, with birds of all colours. Colours that you rarely see in your world. So as the little ones recover, so they will go to this garden for nourishment and joy. I will leave you in the hope that your promises will be kept."

Circle: "They will be."

Chi: "Thank you. Please do not forget the children of the teacher. Go with love into light. Know that all will be well on our side. Peace be with you."

21/03/96 All present. Played 'Little Red Rooster' and meditation after that. Saw a little bit of colour and had a tickling sensation in the palm of my left hand at one point. It was if had a 'cup' made out of stone in the palm of my hand, which was facing downwards. Audrey seemed a bit unsettled, but Mike was very deep. After an hour we closed and had tea and chocolate biscuits, and did our drawings.

28/03/96 All present. Played 'Little Red Rooster' and then had our meditation. Had some pains down my back that didn't help, and didn't sense much. Audrey was in some pain, and it was obviously affecting her. Bernard's telephone ringing also 'woke' people up! We closed after an hour and had tea and cake. Then Bernard announced that he had agreed to sell the house and would be moving fairly shortly. It is a great pity that he is leaving us, but he has been greatly troubled all winter about staying here. No meeting next week as Bernard will be away, as I am.

11/4/96 Just Bernard and myself. Mike and Audrey away in Glasgow. We sat in silence for about forty-five minutes. Nothing at the start as the player has been packed. We then had tea and discussed his moving. It looks like most of the paperwork is nearly finished and he plans to move before the end of the month.

18/04/96 Just Bernard and myself again. I brought my tape recorder, so we had 'Little Red Rooster', and then meditation. Felt quite good with plenty of power around. Also felt that healing was taking place. After fifty minutes we closed the circle and had tea and biscuits. Still one or two minor problems to be sorted before Bernard is away. He gave me almost a full bottle of 'Grouse' whisky.

25/04/96 Last meeting of the 'Willow Circle'! All present. Bernard leaves on Tuesday and the Peacheys have expressed a desire to drop it in favour of healing for the time being. We meditated in silence. Then Chi came through: "Good evening friends. The last day of term has arrived! Over the last few years you have learnt many things. Your eyes, that were once closed, are now open. And it is time to spread the knowledge you now have in other directions. This is meant to be. When you are at school you do not stay in the same class year upon year upon year upon year. Is this not so?"

Circle: "True."

Chi: "You have passed the first stage, now you have got to go and help other people to reach the stage that you are now at. It has got to be. In one particular case, a very gentle, very loving, but, firm within this love. Do you understand? I am speaking to our friend who is leaving."

Bernard: "Yes. Is it possible to make that a little clearer?"

Chi: "You have a daughter?"

Bernard: "Yes."

Chi: "Yes, this is who we speak about."

Bernard: "Gentle and understanding … yes! I understand fully, thank you!"

Chi: "There is still work for you to do."

Bernard: "I look forward to it."

Chi: "Your Earthly years pass so quickly. This you must appreciate. You have not finished learning by any means."

Bernard: "I thirst for knowledge."

Chi: "We know, we know. This is why you must go and pass that knowledge on. The people who you sit with do not need that – you have all learnt. You have all gained knowledge. And there is work also for the rest of you to do, a great deal of work. You may think at times that it is not appreciated, but this is looking inward on yourselves. We need *all* the people that we can muster, to enlighten, even if it is only a glimmer, to those who are seeking. Once the crack has been opened then it may be for others to open it further – but that crack has to be made first of all. Ways are always found to go round. We do not use force – that is not our way. But if there are obstacles ways are found around. The light and the knowledge has to be spread in all directions.

"You will never be apart now that you have been found. One of your kind once said that it is like a secret underground, and we feel this is a very good way of putting it. That you work gently and quietly, then at the right time, the right place, up you pop! You do know that you are all linked together in this knowledge?"

Circle: "Yes."

Chi: "And if one of you needs help – the others will always be there. Iheard you speaking of this place, and you are quite correct when you say that this is a very peaceful home, because you must realise that the energies get soaked into the fabric of this house, and this energy that is around the dwelling place is a very forceful energy. So who enters the home has this energy. They draw from it, they draw peace from any of the homes that are loving and caring. So people go out thinking 'why do I feel so peaceful'? And it is because of the energies that are within the fabric. They are like solid bricks, vibrating away. So though you may physically leave the home, you are always in contact. May I describe it rather like a child's ball on a string. You have the central wooden pivot with elastic attached to the ball. And when it goes out – it always comes back to the centre. So go knowing that you are on another phase."

Bernard: "Thank you."

Chi: "I think you also know that your brother needs you."

Bernard: "Yes I do."

Chi: "Go with Chi - which is energy and service."

Bernard: "Thank you."

Chi: "Don't think you have heard the last of me!"

Circle: "I hope not – I hope we still retain this bond. Perhaps we can also give you our thanks for the many hours of insight and wisdom that you have relayed to us, though we feel there will be further contact."

Chi: "Yes, there will be my friends. Once we have made this contact –

you will find that it is very hard to get rid of us!"

Circle: "I would not wish to!"

Chi: "I will go now. I send you the love of all those that have entered into your circle. I will tell you a little secret. I don't know if I'm allowed to say – whether you will actually be here when it occurs – but that scamp of ours that got reborn, will one day make a very great healer. God bless. Go in love into light. We will meet again."

Circle: "I hope so."

We then had tea and biscuits and a good talk.

That proved to be the last of the circle, though from time to time there were suggestions of maybe forming another circle. However, all of us were busy in all sorts of ways, and so it never happened. Chi continued to be with Audrey. At one of our healing group meetings in September, Audrey told me that Chi was there, but she resisted the temptation to speak. She said that Chi had told her that the Willow Circle had been 'in winter' during the summer, but that it would be spring again and that the leaves would be brighter than ever. Also that Gladys said hello and that baby Geraldine is now trying to be a 'little red rooster' as well!

At the same group later in that month it became clear that Audrey had someone with her. Eventually Chi came though to say that a higher entity had been trying to get through, and that it had taken it out of Audrey a bit. He said there were important teachings to do, and that we must try to teach others. Chi added that 'the twins are doing fine', with a big smile on Audrey's face! I thought this was a reminder that our Willow Circle should be reformed.

At the weekend seminar about a week later, Audrey sat for trance and Chi came through. He was questioned closely, especially over his dress as a Chinese official in his lifetime, it seems someone thought the colour was not right! I relieved the tension near the end by asking whether he missed the Rolling Stones! He laughed and said 'no', but that she did. It was nice to hear his voice again.

The proposition of a development circle was talked about even in the early part of 1997, and despite some in the healing group expressing an interest, getting an evening to suit proved difficult, and the idea eventually withered. Audrey did tell me at that meeting that she had been told that Geraldine was to be reincarnated and that Gladys was trying to come to terms with this.

Meetings with Doris

12/09/99 (Doris 'D', 'M', 'E' and myself present)
After about 5 minutes I asked 'E' if there was anyone with her. She said, "Yes, it's a man and he's not very pleased at being brought here. He didn't want to come. Why have you brought me here? And he doesn't like your music either. I'm sorry, not what he's used to."
    'D': "In that case he's very rude. We don't have to accept rudeness, so I suggest he goes away and comes back, and comes in the spirit that we are inviting him here."
    Me: "Anything else?"
    'E': "He says he's not used to this kind of life."
    'D': "Who brought him here?"
    'E': "He was here before you asked Rasheed. I felt something work up this leg [her left] and I feel that it was like gangrene or something like that, that went up his left leg. And because of what happened when he was here, he didn't want to come back, because of all the suffering and the pain, and he's angry."
    'D': "Why did he come then? Nobody brought him, he must have come on his own accord."
    'E': "Curiosity."
    'D': "Does he need help?"
    'E': "He didn't realise that he needed help, but he does now."
    'D': "Right, we will help him if we can. Will you ask him Mike if – he may find it difficult to understand that I'm suggesting to you what he asks – but somebody close to him will explain why. If he looks round hard enough he will find someone

there, close to him. Does he feel that we can help him move on? Is he drawn to the light that we have sent out? Because the same light he will see close to him, if he really wants help."

Me: "Did he see the light? Is that what drew him to us?"

'E': "Yes!"

Me: "Is he aware of the light round him?"

'E': "He thought he was on his own. He thought he was in a… blackness. He thought he was isolated because of what happened to his leg. That he might spread it to other people."

Me: "Did he lose his leg?"

'E': "It was said at different times that it would be cut off at different places, but it wasn't, and it spread up into his body. His body could not stand any more, of the pain."

Me: "Is he aware of the light round him?"

'E': "He's aware of the light here, and the feelings that are here, and he's beginning to understand … that he doesn't need to be where he is."

'D': "Is he feeling any pain left over from his past life? You ask Mike."

Me: "Is he feeling any pain that he had when he was on earth?"

'E': "Not the physical pain, the resentment, the isolation."

Me: "Can he see now that he is not isolated? Can he see others around him?"

'E': "Dimly, dimly, dimly."

Me: "Can he move towards those shapes, towards those lights? Does he notice them getting brighter?"

'E': "He is noticing that he is better able to move, because he only had one good leg. He is noticing that he can move better."

Me: "Those lights and shapes that he sees will offer him healing."

'E': "He can hear!"

Me: "Good. Can he move towards those lights?"

'E': "He is doing – but it is slow. Because he doesn't know what he is moving towards. He's a bit apprehensive!"

Me: "He's moving towards healing."

'E': "Because of how he was treated when he was here, people didn't want to know him, people kept him away. And he is worried about the reception."

Me: "He is wary."

'E': "Yes!"

Me: "If he holds out his hands, they will hold out their hands towards him. He will not be rejected."

'D': "It is easy to do."

'E': [Very emotional] "No one held out their hand to me! No one wanted to touch me."

'D': "Spirit healers and helpers will. Don't be frightened, just stretch your hands out. We're sending strength to you. Strength, support, compassion and love."

'E': "Why? Why?"

'D': "Because we know what is there for you if you will go towards it. We know the happiness and the peace that you will receive, if you just try to hold both hands out to those shapes that you see, that are lightening the more you concentrate on them."

'E': "Why do you do this for me?"

'D': "Because we want to help you. We have all been through similar things to yourself here on earth, so even if we have not experienced what you have, we can imagine what you have gone through. And we want you to find peace now. You deserve peace. Just give it a try, that is all we are asking."

'E' "Yes."

'D': "We can't work miracles, and we can't do it without your help. But we will give you all the love within us, to help you find the strength and determination, to hold your hand out and move towards them. Just think about it if you can't move – let them know you want to."

'E': "I want to – but I can't believe that people want me!"

'D': "Of course they do. If you go towards them, they will help you, and then you in turn will be able to help others who are in a similar position to yourself, to help them understand. Find the strength to do it, give it a try."

'E': "Yes. I want to."
'D': "We all hold back and then later on could kick ourselves for having done so."
'E': "I've been so lonely."
'D': "You can come and visit us anytime you want. We got off on the wrong foot, because you were rude when you came through, but we understand that rudeness, because we've all been rude to others at some time."
'E': "I'm sorry."
'D': "We're only human, as you were when you were here. So this is why we feel we understand you, and what you're thinking. This is why we feel we can help you and want to help you. You will find help and support, because you are spirit."
'E': "I'm gliding, gliding."
'D': "Is it easy?"
'E': "Quite easy."
'D': "Where are you moving towards? Are the shapes any lighter?"
'E': "They're bigger."
'D': "Then let them know by thought that you want to draw even closer to them, you want them to take your hands. You've got to want them to help you."
'E': "Yes."
'D': "And they will."
'E': "I know."
'D': "If you're sincere they'll help you."
'E': "Oh! I need help."
'D': "Well, you have nothing to lose have you?"
'E': "No."
'D': "I'm going to let Mike talk to you now, because we're trying to help Mike, so that he can help others that come to his groups. So bear with us please, we're asking you to be patient with us too. But keep in your mind the fact that you would welcome the help of those good spirits."
'E': "Yes."
Me: "You say the shapes are getting bigger – are they getting closer?"

'E': "Yes."
Me: "Brighter?"
'E': "Yes."
Me: "Well, keep going towards them."
'E': "They're not terribly bright yet, it is like an outline. I can see an outline, I see a light for the eyes and a light for the mouth."
'D': " Can we explain at this point that it could be, that because he's been in dim light for quite a while, they don't want to cause him any distress by shining too brightly. At this point, as long as he can see them and know they are there, they will get brighter as his eyes adjust to the lighter conditions."
'E': "I can see shoulders … down the side."
Me: "They are there to help you."
'E': "Yes I know, I can feel. I cannot see their hands yet. I cannot … it is just an outline at the moment. But they are getting bigger and they are coming nearer."
Me: "Are you reaching out towards them?"
'E': "Yes. I have my hands out."
Me: "You must ask for help, and they will help."
'E': "Yes. But they know that I am nervous, and so they are coming slowly, so that they don't frighten me."
Me: "That's right. And they will get brighter, you will see more. You will see more as they come towards you. How long have you been away from the earth?"
'E': "I don't know." [crying]
Me; "A long time."
'E': "There wasn't any medication, nothing to make my leg better. They're here!"
Me: "They've come?"
'E': "They are all around me!"
Me: "Good. Do you feel the healing, do you feel the love?"
'E': "I feel the gentleness."
Me: "What is your name?"
'E': "Hugo. Hugo."
Me: "Well Hugo, you no longer need to be alone. They will take

you to a place where they will help you, to recover fully."

'E': "And I thank you all, for being here."

Me: "Not at all. You're welcome back, at any time that you may wish to come."

'E': "That will not be for a while. I don't want to come back here."

Me: "I can understand."

'E': "Not until I am strong."

Me: "But you will get that strength."

'E': "Yes! I'm going now. I'm going."

Me: "Go with our love."

'E': "Thank you. I've had very little love."

Me: "You will have lots now."

'E': [faintly] "Yes – I'm going."

About five minutes later I asked 'E' again if anybody was with her.

'E': "I've got a man. Who was hung. He was hanged for sheep stealing. And he took a sheep to feed his family, and he was hung. I can see the gibbet and him hanging.

Me: "Does he have a name?"

'E': "It must be a surname because I'm getting Arbuthnot, but he is saying 'Arbuthdid'."

Me: "What drew him to us?"

'E': "He was listening. They are saying he wasn't all that bad. He wasn't a wicked man, but he did take that sheep."

Me: "Did he blame himself? Somehow.."

'E': "Yes. He took it. He took it."

Me: "But what is past is past. Does he wish help?"

'E': "He is saying he thought that was all there was, the condition he was in, that was all he was entitled to, because of what he'd done."

Me: "But he now knows different?"

'E': "Yes."

Me: "And he can see the light?"

'E': "Yes, and he now realises that he wasn't so bad really. He had a good reason for doing it. He was told how bad he was, how wicked he was for what he had done."

'D': "Spirit world judge on the thought behind the action and not the action; does he understand?"

'E': "Beginning to understand. He was resigned to being where he was, because he thought that was what he deserved."

Me: "But he realises now that that is not really the case?"

'E': "Hmmm."

Me: "That there's something better."

'E': "He's ... he said being hung is a terrible punishment for what he did."

Me: "Yes it was."

'E': "And then his children had no one to look after them."

Me: "So maybe he blames himself, more than anybody else would blame him. He needs to let go of that."

'E': "Yes."

'D': "Did he kill the sheep and then.."

'E': "Yes. Yes. He's not terribly emotional like the last one. He.."

'D': "He has to move on over the bridge to the next plane."

'E': "Yes."

'D': "They're waiting for him to do that I think."

'E': "And he's ready, he's saying he is ready."

Me: "Good."

'E': "He's ready to go."

Me: "What can he see now?"

'E': "He's on his way."

'D': "They can only come so far, he will have to cross himself the biggest part of the divide."

'E': "He's tried and out, he's on his way."

'D': "And they will take him across the last part. We wish him well."

Me: "Yes. We wish him God speed."

'E': "He's running now. He's running! And arms outstretched."

('E' then broke off and drank water, etc.)

10/10/99 (Doris, 'M', 'E' and myself present)

'D': "I've been joined by ... he tells me his name is Eric. Foster, he said not Forster – Foster. He's looking for John. He said

John can tell him – no – John will take him where he wants to go if he can find John, because John knows all about these things. He said John slipped away – he couldn't hold him, and now he can't find him and he's been looking a long time."

Me: "Did he pass over with John?"

'D': "Yes. They got out, they got out all right. John told me to hang on, but I couldn't. He said it would be alright if I hung on to him, but I couldn't."

Me: "Does he know how long it has been? Has it been a long time? Does it feel like a long time?"

'D': "A long, long time, a long, long time."

Me: "In that case John might be looking for him."

'D': "He hasn't seen him."

Me: "Does he see any light?"

'D': "No. No light. I can answer for myself. Shouldn't have to repeat. The only light is your light."

Me: "Right."

"D': "It was dark then, it is dark now. John said to hold on, we would go to the light."

Me: "John knew what he was doing."

'D': "He knew the way. We laughed at him – but he was sure. He told me to hold on to him, and I couldn't, couldn't, just went."

Me: "Does he want to find the light?"

'D': "It was cold, cold, cold and damp."

Me: "Does he want to find the light?"

'D': "I want to find John! John knows where the light is."

Me: "Yes. But do you .."

'D': "The others have all gone."

Me: "You must need to find the light."

'D': "I need to find John."

Me: "John is probably waiting."

'D': "Why doesn't he call me?"

Me: "John can't do it for you – you have to do it."

'D': "I've been calling John, John, John. I called John."

RESCUE WORK

Me: "Have a good look round, have a good look round."
'D': "John."
Me: "Do you not see anything at all?"
'D': "Too dark, too dark."
Me: "Look very carefully. Pray for the light."
'D': "The light went out with the explosion."
Me: " With the explosion?"
'D'; "Yes."
Me: "You passed very quickly then?"
'D': "Explosion, yes. Everybody went. John was only a lad, but he knew where he was going. He knew where he was going."
Me: "Where was John going?"
'D': "He didn't say. He said hold on to him, and I'd be all right. But I couldn't hold on. Just slipped."
Me: "Where do you think John is?"
'D': "John's where it's warm, where he's safe. He knew where he was going."
Me: "And you want to get there too?"
'D': "I want to find John."
Me: "Well John is waiting."
'D': "Yes, he'll wait for me, he'll wait for me."
Me: "But he can't do it all, you must do some of it."
'D': "They're all gone."
Me: "You must look towards the light, you must want to go towards the light."
'D': "The light went out with the bang."
Me: "Yes, but it will come back if you want it. What do you want, apart from seeing John?"
'D': "I want to get out of this blackness."
Me: "Right."
'D': "And the cold, it's so cold, it's so cold. So cold."
Me: "Can you see nothing around except blackness? No dim shape?"
'D': "Just darkness, cold. We were just left in the dark and the cold. Shouted 'tantivy' but … nobody heard, nobody heard."
Me: "Sorry, nobody heard what?

'D': "We shouted tantivy. TANTIVY WE SHOUTED. SHOUTED TANTIVY, TANTIVY, AND NOBODY HEARD."

Me: "What is tantivy? I'm sorry, I don't know."

'E': "Hunting."

Me: "Hunting? Thank you. I couldn't place it. Well, you must hunt for the light, but you must want the light. And *you* must, John cannot do it for you." [*The tape recording ended at this point.*]

Shortly after this Doris said that he'd gone back. I was upset that we hadn't managed to help him, and I blamed myself, despite my lack of experience of being in charge.

[*There was slight sequel to this. I telephoned Doris several weeks later. She informed me that she had sat and got something regarding Eric Foster. He was very young, only about 19, dressed in overalls and seemed to be situated in the engine room. The John he had been talking about was a John Diamond, some sort of officer, wearing a dark navy uniform with a propeller badge on the sleeve – considered a gem by all who knew him, not only by name but by nature. A friend of mine who had been in the Navy, told me that the badge indicated a 'Stoker'. To have a peaked cap, he would have to be at least a Petty officer; some were known as 'possums': POSM – Petty Officer Stoker Mechanic.*]

A little later Doris spoke, "I'm aware of some people here – 'E'?"

'E': "Just feel as if I'm sleeping, sleeping and sleeping and not getting anywhere. I just feel that it is somebody who is in that state. Being told about limbo, and that's all they expect."

'D': "I think we could do with a little more help from the spirit side, because there are quite a few people here in what 'E' said – limbo – in that state. That they are not aware of where they are, or where they are going."

'E': "I'm seeing some flowers now."

'D': "What kind of flowers?"

'E': "Just like … about six flat petals with the centre standing a bit proud. Think from white to pale pink."

'D': "I'll leave you with that and see if it enlarges on that. 'M' are you, have you any impressions?"

'M': "I've a mother and her daughter, been here for ages. The mother died in childbirth."

'D': "Anything else? It's obvious what they are doing here is giving us ordinary clairaudience, clairvoyance and showing us situations, telling us about situations. So I might have to handle it in a different way. Could be when they ... and I hope my friends are listening to me and will give me a sign if this is right or wrong ... that they are showing us about their experiences, telling us about their experiences, but they don't want to keep thinking about them and reliving them and this is what they seem to be doing. Reliving the experiences of their circumstances of their death. And it could be if we are receptive to that, and we are voicing it for them, they may now be able to put behind them these circumstances."

'M': "I don't want to stay here."

'D': "See the light, and recognise the light, and move on towards it once they have got over, they have relived that experience. They have to get past the stumbling block. You don't want to stay there, no. How did you get there? Tell us how you got there please? Whether it be good or bad, the channel is quite able to take your experience."

'E': "I was ill for a long time, in bed. I just died."

'D': "Was it peaceful or painful?"

'E': "No, it was peaceful. But I just continued as I had been when I was ill, lying, waiting for something to happen."

'D': "And it hasn't yet happened?"

'E': "Those flowers are the first thing that I've seen."

'D': "Well, those flowers probably mean that somebody you can't see yet is offering you flowers. Hope for the future. Are you holding those flowers? Will you take them? Because if you take them ... put your hand out and touch the flowers if you can. If you can touch the flowers, if you can take them and look carefully, feel that there is something special around those flowers. If you can't see a faint glow around them, can you feel any life in those flowers, any energy or.."

'E': "I can touch the petals."

'D': "And you can feel the petals? Well, you should be able to feel the warmth of the glow around the petals around the flowers."

'E': "That's the first thing I've seen for so long."

'D': "Can you see who has given you those flowers? Or whose placed them before you?"

'E': "Small lady. A small lady."

'D': "Will you ask her if you can go with her? What does she say?"

'E': "She's just going." [Making a forward sign with an index finger.]

'D': "Follow her then. Go with her. She knows what she is doing."

'E': "Yes."

'D': "And you will be all right. But make sure that you stay with her until you get where she's taking you. And then you'll find it will be all right. Does it feel good?"

'E': "It feels, it feels as if I'm moving slowly and yet I think I'm going fast. Speeding, but there isn't the sensation of speed."

'D': "You feel safe?"

'E': "Yes, comfortable."

'D': "You should soon arrive at a safe place, where you will find hope for the future."

'E': "Getting lighter."

'D': "Good. And once you see others, do everything they tell you, gladly and willingly. And you will find that things will get even better, because they know what they are about. And they will take you to a place of safety and happiness."

'E': "I feel so weak."

'D': "You will do, that is a natural reaction. You have been waiting some time, to move on to another destination. Just enjoy the weakness."

'E': "I wish I had known more. I wish I had known. I was told so many things. But I now know they weren't true. I didn't want to lay there. Indefinitely. Now, I'm beginning to understand that I didn't need to. I have a cool breeze on my face."

'D': "It will feel nice and pleasant."

'E': "It's ... waking me up. Oh. What a waste of time! What a waste of time. And I'm not stupid!"

'D': "The lady is still there even if you can't see her still. She's still with you."

'E': "Yes."

'D': "Do everything she tells you. Just follow her until you get to where you are going. Will you ask the lady to speak to me please?"

'E': "Yes."

'D': "Just for a little while. I just want to say thanks, I know she's here, I can see her, I just want to say thank you to her for helping you, but I feel there is more to it than this. This lady is showing herself to me. I would like to know why, the reason for it. I'm sure it is a good reason."

'E': "I have watched over this soul for a long time, waiting for her to wake up, and I am grateful for what you have done, or I would still have been trying to get through the misconceptions, the mind closed to the reality of spirit. So I thank you for helping me to help her."

'D': "Thank you friend. I hope to see you again. Perhaps there are others that you will bring to us that need help."

'E': "Yes. There are others like me also who help."

'D': "Ellen. I want to call you or the other lady Ellen, I don't know why. Ellen, not Helen, Ellen. Is there a reason for this? Or is it just a passing name?"

'E': "I was not Ellen."

'D': "Was the lady you helped?"

'E': "We can call her that. It doesn't matter."

'D': "No. I'm just wondering you see if Ellen ... perhaps somebody will tell us later."

'E': "I was Florence Margaret, known as Margaret, but my name was Florence Margaret."

'D': "Thank you for that Florence. May we leave you to get on with your work now, and thank you very much for having joined us."

'E': "Thank you."

'D': "And taking care of your channel."
Doris told 'E' to drink some water, and then said, "Now then 'M', what is your visitor/friend telling you? Any more? She died in childbirth."
'M': "I'm jut so weary."
'D': "Yes, you will be. Have you been in the spirit world long?"
'M': "A while, yes."
'D': "Have you been able to take a look yet at your family, or have you not yet had that opportunity to see how they are faring?"
'M': "Nobody wants to know me."
'D': "In spirit or on earth? You died in childbirth, did the child survive?"
'M': "Yes."
'D': "Would you not like to take a look?"
'M': "I've seen her."
'D': "You've seen her. Did somebody take you to see her?"
'M': "No, she came to see me."
'D': "She came to see you … in her thoughts or has she passed over too?"
'M': "She's passed over. She was a little darling."
'D': "That would be a pleasure for you."
'M': "It was."
'D': "What is her spirit name?"
'M': "Helen."
'D': "Helen or Ellen?"
'M': "Helen."
'D': "The little girl will now be in a nice part of the spirit world, all children are. Why haven't you followed her? Has anyone offered to take you?"
'M': "No."
'D': "Why do you think this is?"
'M': "'Cause I was naughty."
'D': "Well, that is all past now. No need for you to think about that, I'm sure you've thought about it long enough."
'M': "Yes."
'D': "Since you did pass over, so perhaps it's time to put all that

behind you now, and move forward. Then you will be able to visit your daughter again, and see how she's progressing, rather than her have to come to visit you. Because she will be very sad seeing you haven't moved on. So wouldn't it be nice if you could move on?"

'M': "Yes."

'D': "And you could both meet in the same pleasant surroundings. Why not give it a try? Concentrate on moving, really into the Summerland."

'M': "I see trees."

'D': "Try to go closer towards them into the Summerland of the spirit world. Even if you can't see someone, there will be a spirit there. Maybe more than one, waiting to help you, to give you confidence and the courage to keep moving forward until you reach the Summerland. It only takes a little courage, that is all that is required. Just the wish and the will to move in the right direction. Are you making progress along the way?"

'M': "Yes."

'D': "I'll now leave you in the safe hands of those who are about you, and wish you well on the rest of your journey. We know that you will get there and be very happy there. Perhaps when you've settled you may like to join us again to let us know how you are getting on in your new environment, a much happier, pleasanter place. Thank you for joining us."

After a short discussion, Doris said, "I'm being told now that we have to use a different candle. And the words that are being used are attempted, Attempted Rescue. And that whilst it is healing work, it is of a different nature. Got to keep the candle lit, whilst attempting rescue work. And we have to get rid of the words 'rescue work' – we are helping lost souls."

'M': "I've a gentleman here, came in airforce uniform, and he just wants to say thank you for rescuing that lady, because he's tried for ages. Because he was the one that was at fault, and she wouldn't go. Now she's gone, and thank you."

'D': "Thank you friend, thank you for telling us this."

Doris then explained that once they have started to go, we can break the link, drink water and then we are ready to receive anybody else. Then it was repeated for Doris – helping lost souls. 'E' said she had heard 'Onward Christian Soldiers', and Doris related that that had been going in the background when the first person came through – the man in the submarine. Lots of military people today. Then we discussed what had happened. Doris thought it was not really 'rescue' work, more like 'getting something off your chest' to move forward.

7/11/99 (Doris, 'C', 'E' and myself present)
> 'E' then got a picture of a dark haired girl sitting in front of the fire, she had a fringe cut down at the sides, and she was just sitting there. She was taking something out of a parcel. "At first I thought it was a skateboard, but she would have been too young for it."

'D': "How old is she?"
'E': "I would say about two and a half to three."
'D': "What is she here for?"
'E': "Because she wants to see Christmas, and all the things for Christmas."
'D': "Did somebody bring her?"
'E': "I didn't see anybody with her, but I will ask. She's just saying the nice lady brought her."
'D': "We've nothing Christmassy, but we could show her.."
'E': "She's been to the shops she says. She's been to see the shops, with all the decorations and the toys. She died before she could open her Christmas presents."
'D': "Right. Well hold her with you, keep her here, and we'll see if we can find her something for Christmas." [Doris then left to rummage in a box – got a glass night light thing with nice colours.]
'E': "She likes the candle and the fire."
'D': "Still holding her 'E'?"
'E': "She's sitting on my knee now."

'D': "Have you got a name for her?"
'E': "I asked, but she says she couldn't remember if she was a Mary or Margaret, and it was a long time ago."
'D': "Right, here's a little Christmas light especially for her, and we'll play a tune for her and she can watch the lady go round." [A wind-up rotating lady that played a tune.]
'E': "She's tearful now."
'D': "I wish her a happy Christmas and ask her to accept the tune and the candle as a gift from us with love."
'E': "She's saying she went on the fire."
'D': "She's all right now though. Thank her for coming to us as she was when she passed over, and we hope that she can go on now, to grow up and progress well in the spirit world."
'E': "She looks a well-cared for child. She's saying I'm fifteen really."
'D': "Is she?"
'E': "I missed all those birthdays."
'D': "We will treat her visit today as a birthday as well as Christmas, and she can celebrate all the birthdays that she's missed. We'll let her go on now with the lady that brought her, so she can now move on and progress. And is able to come again, we will welcome her in a month's time, and we can get a little news from her then."
'E': "Thank you."

Doris then asked 'C' if anybody was there with her; 'C' didn't know – but felt there was some sort of contraption in her hands, like a double rolling pin.

'D': "Why do you think they have placed that in your hands?"
'C': "Something I used to work with."
'D': "Were you a cook? A baker?"
'C': "Yeah! A kitchen."
'D': "What do you feel like in stature?"
'C': "Larger than what I am, but I'm not aware of any sex, either male or female. Quite big hands. Possibly a heavy woman I think."

'D': "Now, how do you feel you are dressed? Start with your feet, your shoes."

'C': "My feet feel quite heavy. I don't know about shoes, but I feel the clothing is down to my feet. That's quite heavy. Don't know about colour. Just sort of negative image."

'D': "What about round the neck.."

'C': "I feel there's something on my head, possibly tied at the back as it feels quite tight."

'D': "A scarf of some sort or a hat with a tie. Is this to keep your hair in?"

'C': "I think so, because it's quite long."

'D': "Have you got long sleeves, short sleeves?"

'C': "I feel quite covered up all over."

'D': "Now take a look at what's about you. Or do you feel you are in this room, dressed as you were in this life? Just think about it."

'C': "I'm getting a vision of a kitchen. There's a fireplace, looks like a working fireplace."

'D': "A range?"

'C': "Ahha…there's a window, sink, a small house, a home."

'D': "What happened in this home? Ask her, because she's showing you that for a reason."

'C': "It's very bare."

'D': "Ask her why she's showing you this."

'C': "There's no children."

'D': "Husband, parents?"

'C': "No, she's…it's her home."

'D': "So she's on her own. Why is she on her own? Is she a widow or a spinster?"

'C': "Husband's not there."

'D': "Temporarily, or has he left her?"

'C': "I think it's temporary, for it's as if she's waiting. I'm getting sensations in my legs – bad circulation, swelling. Isolated, it's not in a village or a town. It's not a farm."

'D': "The condition of the legs – is that an ongoing thing, has she been troubled long?"

'C': "I get the feeling it's ongoing. It has to do with weight."
'D': "Try to find out how she passed over. This is what she is trying to tell you."
'C': "The letter 'T'."
'D': "What is it then?"
'C': "It's a nail."
'D': "A nail?"
'C': "Ahha!"
'D': "Ask why a nail."
'C': "It's a blacksmith."
'D': "Now I'm going to speak to her direct 'C', and I want you to answer what comes into your mind. I'm hoping she will answer using your voice."
'C': "It was quick."
'D': "Was it a normal illness? Was the ongoing complaint with your legs the cause of your death?"
'C': "I think so."
'D': "Can you give me an approximate time, year?"
'C': "17…"
'D': "Yes, the 18th century, that's near enough. Did a doctor attend you?"
'C': "No."
'D': "What are you doing now in the spirit world? Or are you just staying close to your old home, or the image of your old home?"
'C': "Just waiting."
'D': "Waiting for what?"
'C': "Waiting for someone."
'D': "Who are you waiting for – someone you knew or someone to help you?"
'C': "Someone to come near."
'D': "You do know that you have passed on – no doubt about that? You do accept that? Do you?"
'C': "Yeah."
'D': "Yes? In that case now you have to leave behind the images of your life at the home where you lived, and your illness, and

ask for someone to take you onto another level. Someone will come. You may see only a small speck of light. Move towards it if you can, or ask them to help you to move towards it, and you will go on from there. If you want to that is. How do you feel about that?"

'C': "They've gone! I felt very lightheaded."

'D': "At what point did they move?"

'C': "Realisation, about talking about how she passed over, she realised she had passed and ... physically I felt very lightheaded and then very light, and then just back here!"

'D'; "Just sit still, don't move. [Doris looking carefully] Okay, take a drink now 'C'."

That was the last 'Rescue work' that occurred, as the meetings became more infrequent due to the deterioration in the health of Doris.

Closed Circle

The circle at this stage consisted of only four people, 'X', 'Y', 'Z' and myself. We sat under red light that had a dimmer switch, that spirit often altered according to their inclination or desire. In the circle meeting previous to where this account begins, spirit talked about angels and then continued, "We ask you, to use this to help those that are less fortunate in the spirit world. For they will come to seek guidance from each of you, to help, to show them the way they are meant to go, both spiritually and materially."

29/11/07 'Z' said he got quite strongly that a Sister of Mercy was standing between himself and 'Y'. There were one or two people with her from a war-torn country. He could see a family, a young woman with a headscarf and her elderly mother with a similar covering, also a man and some children. It seems they were caught up in tragic circumstances and 'went' very quickly. The area was like Budapest or somewhere round about that region. They looked as if they could do with some help to move on.

While 'Z' had been talking I noticed that 'Y's hands, especially the left one, were moving. So I asked her if anyone was with her. 'Y' said there was somebody pulling her hands, they kept twitching, but that she couldn't get a sense of who the person was.

    'Z' then mentioned that he had sensed a funny smell, like a gas or something, but could not identify it. He still saw the family. 'X' then reported that the mother was now happy and had got the children, and they were walking up the gradient in the corner between her and 'Z'. I asked if there were steps, but 'X' was sure it was just a gradient upwards. 'Z' said that the Sister of Mercy was now smiling and going with them. 'X' thought that maybe the country was Romania as she got that the children were from an orphanage in Romania.

We then opened out again. After a bit 'Z' related that he saw somebody, rather like a monk, sitting cross-legged, who was saying we needed to ask if there was anybody with us, if there was anything required, and then see what comes. I said that I didn't understand. 'Z' then replied that we had to ask our higher selves and wait and see what comes, as opposed to…if there was anyone wanting to come through or needing help. This man was saying that we needed to ask. Then also, "and you will feel better too!" directed at me (I hadn't been feeling well that day).

So we went with that advice. After a bit 'Z' mentioned that he heard water, but none of the rest of us could. Another lapse of time and then 'X' stated that she saw a young man sitting down and leaning against a tree, lost. He was oblivious to her questions. 'Z' enquired if he needed any help. 'X' said that he didn't know where he was, but she couldn't get him to notice us as he had his head down and knees up. 'Z' asked how 'X' felt he had passed over, to which she replied that it had been quick, but not an illness. Then she said that he didn't really know that he had passed over. 'Z' asked if he was about 17 or 18, which 'X' confirmed and also said he was wearing checked, wooly brown tweed trousers.

'Y' then spoke about getting the name of 'Eric'. 'X' said it could be while ago, as the style looked around the 1950s. 'Z' then asked spirit to use the red light to respond to his questions – but got no response. After a while 'Z' stated that the young man was looking for his father, so maybe his father could come and collect him. A couple of minutes later 'Z' said he had got a connection to the forces, and that it was over 20 years that he had been like that. 'X' thought it was much more and also mentioned that he had a pushbike wherever he went; thought that his father could be called 'Stan'. She said that there was water in front of him, like a stream, and that she was trying to get him interested in that, to get his head raised. 'Z' said we needed to send someone to him to get him up and take him to the light, and then he could get his connection to his dad. 'Z' then asked me to ask someone to go towards that young man. I said that there should be somebody with him, like the Sister of Mercy with the others.

After a minute 'Z' said he doesn't seem to be at the tree, and didn't know where he had gone, but 'X' said he was still there. Then followed a discussion on what could be done. 'Y' said that she felt 'they' were holding him back, keeping him there. The others agreed. 'Y' then asked the 'friend' to let go of him and let him go towards the light. 'X' was asked to send him reassurance. She then mentioned that he had his hands out and was going into the light. She also said that he must have hurt his leg before he passed. Then all agreed that he had gone to the light. [*Subsequently both 'Y' and 'X' disclosed that it was the young man's mother that was holding him back.*]

Reflecting on this circle later, I decided to make a list of topics for discussion at the start of the next circle:

1. *Apologies for being 'out of it' at last meeting; although I wasn't feeling great it was mostly due to tiredness.*
2. *Sister of Mercy and family. We didn't actually do much; maybe they just needed a little bit of love and reassurance from obviously earthy people? 'Y' had someone pulling her hand – one of the children? Finally – not saying this happened – but it came to me that we must guard against assumptions, not all orphans come from Romania.*
3. *Crossed-legged monk. If we all link into our higher selves, what happens if two or three come at the same time?*
4. *Young man. Mea culpa – I didn't give my feelings on this: I felt that the water was a canal, and that the young man may have committed suicide.*
5. *During our discussion afterwards the 'door' came up. Why is it important that the door be closed?*

6/12/07 First we had a brief discussion on the notes I'd made. When discussing number 3, I suggested that when one person said that they had somebody with them, and another of the group also had a person with them, then that other person should *not* try to link in with the others, but try to maintain that link until the others had dealt with the first one, then we could deal with the second together. All agreed. On number 5, 'Y' explained that the door was closed because the room was also used for different purposes at different times. Then the circle was opened.

After about four minutes 'X' said she was aware of a door, an old wooden door in a hallway. The door was just opened a little bit and it looked like an old pantry. There was a little old lady – who was like a mouse – cowering behind a door.

> Me: "Is she afraid?"
> 'X': "Yes."
> Me: "Can you get a sense of why she is afraid?"
> 'X': "I get a feeling it is something like a pantry where food was kept, because I can see shelves with pies and that. It's quite a long time ago. It's like 'below stairs'."
> Me: "Was she hungry?"
> 'X': "I think so. It's the master she is frightened of."
> Me: "Was she found out and punished?"
> 'X': "I don't know. She won't come from behind this door for love nor money! She's only…I don't think she's even five foot tall, very skinny, with like…grey and brown clothes on."
> Me: "So she probably wasn't stealing for herself, but for her family?"
> 'X': "I don't know. She was hungry."
> Me: "If you try to send a little love, maybe she will at least acknowledge us. ('Z' indicated he wanted to speak.) Yes, 'Z'."
> 'Z': "I got the name 'Hilda' at the beginning."
> Me: "Right, well you can ask Hilda if she would like to speak to us."
> 'Z': "I know she's got a family and that they are there trying to reach her, but she's got to make the move."
> Me: "Yeah. She's obviously very afraid."
> 'X': "Like a mouse." 'X' then tried to remind us about an actress – without success – who was rather strange looking and had wee button eyes, as the lady had a similar face.
> 'Z': "Ask if she'll go to the light."
> 'X': "Do you get any feelings about the name of Dorothy? As I feel that Dorothy means something to her."
> Me: "Well, it could be a daughter or sister or.."

'Z': "I was going to say a family member."

Me: "And if this Dorothy is a family member, maybe she will help entice her out into the light."

'X': "She has got to be told, be reassured that this master isn't gonna…"

Me: "Yeah."

'X': "That's why she won't come out."

Me: "Well the master is not there any more, and if she would just have a look she'd know. She's quite safe, and there is a lot of love being sent to her, and there are people wanting her, who know her, they've been looking for her. She needs to move on – but she needs to make the first move. She needs to have some courage."

'X': "She's just whimpering like a little…kitten or something."

Me: "Otherwise she'll stay there. Ask her if she can see any light."

'X': "Can we ask for Dorothy to come for her?"

Me: "Yes."

'X': "I think that's the only way she's…"

Me: "She needs somebody to reassure her first."

'Z': "There is definitely somebody waiting by the door."

Me: "Well, can we ask that person?"

'X': "Can we not get, put…just hold a hand out for her?"

Me: "Yeah, to make themselves known, to reassure her, to send her love, and ask her to step towards that light and love and her friends. For the time of being frightened is past. There are people waiting who love her. What's she doing now?"

'X': "She's just having a craic [*Irish word meaning 'banter' or 'chat'*] with her. She's got hold of my hand now."

Me: "Oh good! Reassure her and ask her if she will go to her friend. We come to help her. Her family and friends are waiting for her, to welcome her."

'X': "She's seeing somebody."

Me: "Is she ready to go?"

'X': "She's gone through now."

Me: "Good, good. Thank that friend who came. Okay?"

'X': "Do you close the door 'Z'?"

Me: "Well, we are working, so we will leave it open."

'Z': "They will close it for her, but in the meantime it is open for anyone to use. The door will be closed in the end. It's closed at the moment, she's gone off into the light."

Me: "Have you anybody?"

'Y': "No."

Then I asked the circle to relax again. After about a minute I asked 'Z' if he sensed somebody.

'Z': "I've a feeling of a lot of energy, more than anything at the moment."

Me: "Right."

'Z': "Yeah, I'm cold, surrounded here (indicating his legs), very cold; between me and 'Y' as well. Whether 'Y's got that same feeling I don't know. Energy, the presence of spirit strongly, the lights have just gone down as well."

Me: "I can feel the energy as well."

'Z': "The energy is changing. Whether they are trying to draw close to us to say something, or they're bringing one or two people in for help…but I'm not able to link in at the minute."

Me: "Okay."

After a few minutes:

Me: "Does anybody feel anything? 'Z'?"

'Z': "There was someone, I can just see them building up, I can see someone in a wheelchair. I thought at first it was David, but it isn't."

Me: "Right."

'Z': "The reason I know is that whoever this person is, has got a lovely little…oh, what's the breed?"

Me: "Dog?"

'Z': "A Yorkshire terrier, I can see that very clear. It's a woman. I can just make out the wheelchair, but it's not her that wants the help, she's wanting to bring in somebody."

Me: "Right."

'Z': "Ah…for help, in some way. That's as far as I can get. Whether 'Y' or 'X' or yourself can pick up on that or…"
'X': "Is there a man she's wanting to bring in?"
'Y': "Mmmmm." [*Agreeing*]
'X': "Is it a man?" Both 'Z' and 'Y' said yes.
'X': "A cantankerous old bugger!"
'Z': "Well I wouldn't know about that, but I know that there's a man, that's as far as I can get."
Me: "Can you link in to that 'X'?"
'X': "I've had a man here, taking a bit of a paddy [*Fit of temper*]."
Me; "What's he on about?"
'X': "He's slightly drunk."
Me: "Right."
'X': "And he's called Jack. It's a bit frightening."
Me: "He's frightening?"
'X': "It's a bit frightening."
'Z': "Well, tell him to offski!" [*Get away*]
Me: "Yeah. Calm down, otherwise we can't help him."
'Z': "We don't want that. Now leave 'X' alone!"
Me: "He has to behave himself. 'Y', how about you?"
'Y': "I've got a man she was wanting to help. He wasn't drunk by any means."
Me: "He wasn't?"
'Y'; "Drunk."
Me: "Okay. Can you still get a sense of that man? No? 'X', have you still got him, this cantankerous fellow?"
'X': "Yes. Just like…took a step back. He's got one of these built up shoes on one foot."
Me: "Right, so he's slightly deformed."
'X': "It's just about an inch built up. And he's got a white cloth around his neck. One of them hanky things."
Me; "Yeah. Is he a working man then?"
'X': "Yeah. I think on the docks or something."
'Z': "Well tell him to stay where he is, and to withdraw."
Me: "We might help him yet, you never know. This person has come for him. There was a build up of energy there [*Indicating*

the space beside 'Z'] before you got the wheelchair, so she's come from the light."

Me: "yeah…so.."

'Z': "But she doesn't want to know him."

'Y': "No! To me no! Mine's a different…the person in the wheelchair yes – but it's a different man."

Me: "Alright. Okay."

'Y': "We've got crossed wires."

Me: "We have."

'Z': "I didn't think that the person who was in the wheelchair was connected to him."

Me: "Right."

'Z': "But we can't get…the other man has gone now."

'Y': "He was a gentle man, tall, slimmish, not well built, and he was dressed in a suit."

Me: "In a?"

'Y': "A suit. It was a gentleman. I feel this lady is a bit.."

'Z': "I just heard somebody saying.."

'Y': "Hold on."

'Z': "Carry on 'Y', sorry."

'Y': "Just building up – still there…you're welcome… got a connection here."

'Z': "Just as you were describing the gentleman there, I heard a woman saying, "Yes, that is my Charles"."

Me: "Right."

'Z': "That is my Charles – wasn't Charley or anything – it was 'my Charles'."

Me: "Right. Can you get a sense of this Charles?"

'Y': "He is a very gentle person, very gentle, very loving."

'Z': "I'm getting rather puzzled. Who is it that is needing help then?"

Me: "Well, we'll see. Is this Charles..?"

'Z': "If he is gentle, what's wrong, what's the help for?"

Me: "I'll just see. Does he feel…does he know where he is?"

'Y': "It's as though he's sitting in a chair at home. Oh! I feel he died suddenly."

Me: "So he may not have realized he's dead?"

'Y': "No. No. But she does. Oh! Certainly yes, thank you! Right. Right. Well take his hand. Take him with you. I will reassure him he is safe and when he is, take him to the light. I just want to cry!"

Me: "Has he gone now? Has she taken him to the light?"

'Y': "Yeah."

Me: "Good."

'Y': "They were not tears of sadness, but tears of joy. We're together."

Me: "Good. Now 'X', do you still have that man?"

'X': "He's crying. Sitting at a table, with his arm on the table and his head on his arm."

Me: "Good. Can you get a sense of anybody who is waiting for him? Maybe anybody close to him?"

'X': "I don't think his family want to know him."

'Y': "I feel…will you tell me if I am wrong…that he's like a vagabond."

Me: "Oh. Right."

'X': "He's certainly rough, rough in the mouth and rough looking. He's been a bad 'un."

Me: "A loner. Right, well I think.."

'Y': "We need to help him."

Me: "We need to help him, and if he's got no friend then we need help from.."

'Z': "What we need to do is to get him to face the light, get him to go towards that door."

'Y': "There will be friends."

Me: "Right. What we.."

'X': "I'm a bit scared of him like."

Me: "No! No! You have nothing to be scared of. Ask him to look up and see if he can see any light."

'Y': "Come on. You've got to move."

'Z': "Hold my hand if you want." [*This to 'X'*]

'Y': "He's safe. We're here to help you."

'Z': "Here hold my hand 'X'. Right, now, you tell him to look for that light and he can't or will not harm you. Now, remember, like attracts like, you mustn't allow any negativity, or any emotion to come into play."

'X': "Yep."
'Z': "Right?"
'X': "Yep."
'Z': "Take my hand again."
'X': "No. I'm alright."
'Z': "You're sure?"
'X': "Yep."
'Z': "Are you happy now?"
'X': "Yeah."
'Y': "Has he moved 'X'?"
'X': "No…it's because I've hung back, you see."
'Y': "Right. Tell him…"
Me: "Tell him to look for.."
'Z': "Tell him to look towards the direction of the light."
Me: "Yeah."
'Z': "Over your shoulder."
Me: "Can he see the light?"
'Z': "What's happening?"
'X': "He's sorry now for what he's done."
'Z': "Right."
Me: "That's a good first step, but he needs to look up, he needs to go to the future. Ask him to look up and see the light. Can he see it now?"
'X': "Yeah, he must do, for he's saying a prayer now. He's got his hat in his hand."
Me: "Tell him to walk towards the light and there will be people there to greet him. If he just steps towards the light there will be people there to help him. Ready to help him. Only too willing. That the life he had is passed and there's a brighter future awaiting him, if he just steps towards the light. There are people there ready. Yes?"
'Y': "Is he gone 'X'?"
'X': "Yep! He was just like – sucked through!"

'Y'; "Mmmmm, it was just – whoosh!"
'X': "Just sucked through."
'Y': "We wish him well."
Me: "Now bring your own awareness back. [*Then to 'X'*] And just let that go. Take a drink of water."
'Z': "Don't link in anymore 'X', that's enough. Okay?"
'X': "Yeah."
'Z': "Now, are you absolutely sure you're okay?"
'X': "Yeah, I'm okay."
Me: "Good."
'Z': "You feel drained?"
'X': "No. I hid behind a curtain at the beginning."
'Z': "Just frightened?"
'X': "Aye."

Then followed a short discussion on what 'X' felt and 'Z' giving advice.

Me: "We'll just…ah…there might be one more before we close. Oh, I feel the energy changing."
'Z': "A bit warmer."
'Y': "I've got a fisherman here."
Me: "Right."
'Y': "He's right in the middle of the river. He's fully rigged up for it."
'Z': "Have you just got the one fisherman?"
'Y': "Mmmmm."
'Z': "Because I'd two before…unless one is looking for the other."
Me: "There's a lot of energy around my head. Can you contact this person, can he hear you, can he see you?"
'Y': "I can see him!"
'Z': "Is there still one fisherman 'Y'?"
'Y': "Mmmmm.
'Z': "I get the feeling, as I had two before.."
'Y': "There's something happened."
'Z': "Well, I feel, I could be wrong, I feel that they both went together, but as they went together, got lost."

'Z': "I feel as though he is stuck in the middle of this river. Well, he can't move."
Me: "Right, so we have to give him help."
'Y': "Mmmmm. He daren't move."
'Z': "He can't move?"
'Y': "No."
'Z': "How, is he stuck?"
'Y': "Just stood there."
'Z': "But he'll not move himself?"
'Y': "No, he daren't move."
'Z': "He's rooted to the spot?"
'Y': "Mmmmm."
'Z': "Fear? Would it be fear that's causing it?"
Me: "Right, we need to be sending a little bit of love and.."
'Y': "I'm asking him to take a step, he won't take a step, he daren't. Oh my dear, now come on…okay…come towards us. Try and turn round, gently, slowly, come on. He's beginning to turn round, but very slowly."
Me: "That's okay."
'Y': "To face the bank."
Me: "That's okay, just take it slowly, with plenty of reassurance."
'Y': "Come on, you're safe."
'Z': "I get the feeling that someone is coming to take him by the hand."
'Y': "There is."
Me: "Good."
'Y': "But he's very slow, very slow. I'm trying to think what's happened."
Me: "Is his friend there now?"
'Y': "There is somebody on the bank waiting for him."
Me: "Right. Has he turned round now?"
'Y': "Yes. He's coming towards this other…yes it's a gentleman as well."
Me: "Good. Tell him to take it easily and slowly."
'Y': "Yeah, come on, you're nearly there."
Me: "Try to get to the bank."

'Y': "He's there."
Me: "He's there?"
'Y': "Mmmmm, he's gone up the bank."
Me: "Good. His friend, has he met his friend now?"
'Y': "Mmmmm."
'Z': "Yeah."
Me: "Are they going towards the light?"
'Z': "Yes."
Me: "Yes?"
'Y': "Mmmmm."
Me: "Good."
'Z': "They've gone in. I've just seen them. Gone through now."
'Y': "They're together. Oh that's awful! Sorry about that, it wasn't awful, but it was awful to see him stuck there – rigid."
Me: "There was a lot of energy around there."
'Z': "Oh aye."
Me: "A lot! Right I think that.."
'Z': "That was quite powerful, different type of energy there."
Me: "If we just take our awareness back. And send our thanks to those who have come to help, and to those behind the scenes who have helped us."

Reflecting on the last circle, I made another sheet of notes for discussion at the start of the next one:

1. *Too much talking over one another. This leads to people not saying things fully, leads to change of direction, leads to confusion. All guilty.*
2. *Interestingly we had two people come through who were very much afraid – for different reasons. The wee lady Hilda needed plenty of reassurance before she could move forward. The last person, the fisherman, was similar. He was rooted to the spot with fear, and needed a massive dose of reassurance before he could even begin to move his feet. Even I was aware [being the least sensitive in the group] of the massive amount of energy given by spirit in this case; I don't think we could have done this just by ourselves.*
3. *The woman in the wheelchair. This is where we got 'crossed wires', partly due to No 1, but also because we didn't link in with this first statement from*

'Z'; I should have concentrated on this aspect and we would have been led directly to 'Charles'. 'X' did well to hang on to 'Jack', BUT this was a tester for her, and she must put aside these emotions. We don't have the luxury to be 'emotional' in this situation. There is far worse to come in the future, and we must learn **now** if we wish to continue in this work. It was interesting that he was 'sucked into the light'. I think spirit was just waiting for him, and when he made the first move by praying – they didn't hang about, but took him before he changed his mind!

Person: A good description will indicate their social status, maybe their job, any illness that they had prior to passing, a deformity that could have affected them psychologically, etc. What are their circumstances **now**? Have they come with somebody who needs help? Have they come as a friend to help another? If so who? Can they tell us or show us?
OR If they need help, are they afraid? If so, why? Can we take away that fear or reassure them? Do they know that they are dead? Are they too self critical, maybe due to a sense of honour, family etc.?

13/12/07 We discussed my sheet of notes – all seemed to agree with the points that I'd raised. The circle then was opened, going through our usual sequence.
    Me: "We ask those who have passed over, those who are lonely, lost or bewildered, or those who may be unsure, may they come – even to look and listen, to see what is happening – as we open ourselves up to help those particular people, those souls who are not yet guided to the light for whatever reason. And we ask those in spirit now to help us."
    Me: "Have you anybody with you 'Z'?"

'Z' then related that he had Bluebell, a spirit helper, with him and that there were others near the circle, talking about another called Matthew in particular. I then asked 'Y' the same question.

    'Y': "Mmmmm, right from the start. A coalman, his name is 'Archer'. A leather thing on his back and wearing clogs. He's been dead a while, in the 1940s I would say. On a wagon, delivering coal, and this was his busy time of year. And something happened with his head – my head is just – ooh!"

Me: "He was killed instantly was he?"

'Y': "Oh! Ahh! Oh hell! I don't want that! Don't give it to me!"

Me: "I'll just quickly check with 'X' before we go any further; 'X' have you got anything?"

'X': "Yeah."

Me: "Is it connected?"

'X': "No. No. Not connected. I've had this from the very beginning. First of all, as soon as we started, I could see a pair of hands. They were clasped in front of somebody, one hand on top of the other. But, that wasn't somebody wanting help, that was somebody standing to the right of us, with a long blue gown on, and he was silently observing, his hands were crossed in front of him. I would say he was standing guard as much as observing, but observing in a very formal manner. And then right away, I got this young lad in. it's a young negro, and he'd only be about fifteen, and he's sitting on the floor, and I can just see bare arms, bare chest, bare legs. And he's got one knee up and he's got his arms round his knee and his face is absolutely tear-stained, sobbing his eyes out. And he's wanting his mam, as well."

Me: "Oh, right! Okay, can you hold onto him?"

'X': "Yeah."

Me: "Okay 'Y'?"

'Y': "Mmmmm. I've still got him."

Me: "I noticed that."

'Z': "Right across my shoulder blades, something happened to him very quickly, and he doesn't rightly know where he is yet."

'Y': "He's still delivering coal bags, he thinks he's still delivering coal."

'Z': "He thinks he's still here, in the living. He hasn't understood…"

'Y': "Going on the rounds. Going round and round on those rounds as he went on."

Closed Circle

'Z': "Oh! It's there again!"

Me: "Right. So he's passed over. He's obviously had a very serious accident, maybe very sudden. And he's looking for his mother – is that correct?"

'Y': "Mmmmm. Mmmmm."

'Z': "I'm trying to establish how he passed – but I know he's not giving it to me because he doesn't want to remember it."

Me: "Yeah, that's fine. Just let it go then. Just let it go 'Z'."

'Z': "I'm trying to." ['Z' *was then talking quietly to the man*]

Me: "Have you got his attention 'Y'?"

'Y': "I've just got a nurse that's popped in on the left hand side here. And she's taken hold of his hand." ['Y' *talking to him in a whisper*]

Me: "Is he on his way?"

'Y': "He's just turned round and said, "Thank you"."

Me: "Well that's good, that's good. We wish him well."

'Y': "He's quite happy to go with this nurse."

Me: "Good, we thank that person, whoever it is. Now 'X'?"

'X': "I'm just sitting quietly comforting this young lad. He says his name is 'Ben', and he's very, very upset, very distraught."

Me: "Do you know why?"

'X': "He's been treated badly. He was treated badly, and he escaped from somewhere, where they'd rounded him up. And he was separated from his mam, and he doesn't know where his mam is. And…he's totally on his own now, he knows he's totally on his own."

Me: "Have you any idea of the time?"

'X': "A long time ago. It's more like, em, when you know, there were slaves."

Me: "That's what I was thinking of."

'X': "His skin is very dusty and his face all tear-stained."

'Z': "I was just going to say that his mother is in spirit, and also a brother."

Me: "So he's maybe staying because of his family."

'X': "Just lost! There is nothing around him. It's like a desert, there's no houses or anything. But he has a memory of like a…hut thing, an igloo-type hut thing, with his mam standing in the door. She's quite a stout woman, with her hands on her hips, and that's his memory, that he's looking for."

Me: "Well, maybe if we can ask, maybe his mother, or one of his family to come through to try and encourage him to take that step over. Because, he's been there for some time and he needs to move on, and find that there is a better place than where he is at the moment. Can you convince him to.."

'X': "He's just rocking, and quietly like, wailing."

Me: "But 'X', you need to tell him mentally to look for that light, he needs to make the move."

'X': "I've just been holding on to him while you got the other sorted."

'Z': "I'm convinced his mother is there waiting, but he's also got a brother, and his brother is there waiting for him as well. You need to tell him, to sort of say, look, they know you're upset, etc., etc., but try not to be and start looking for that light. He needs to make some sort of move and then.."

'X': "He still thinks that he can't move, that he's tied down."

'Z': "I know that sweetheart, but that's where you step in, that is where you gently persuade him, to reassure him that he is not like that. You're to break that…that link with him…if you can. You have to reassure him that he's not…just like the coalman, he thought he was still here but he isn't, that's why he moved on."

Me: "I'll just ask you 'Y' if you have anything?"

'Y': "I've got something, but I couldn't tell you who he is. Very shaky."

Me: "Do you think it is linked in?"

'Y': "No."

Me: "So let's deal with this young man. So send love and reassurance, for he needs reassurance. Try and convince him that…mm… we need to actually get him to actively look for his mother and his brother. They are there. The light and help is waiting for him, but he must make the first move. Because sitting there in despair will not do anything for him. His relations are there waiting for him, but they are waiting for him to recognise that they're there. There is help for him."

'X': "I've got the feeling that there is somebody called 'Ruby'. And I think that it could be his mam. She's trying to sing to him."

Me: "Good. Can he hear the singing?"

'X': "I think he's trying to…if he'd just stop rocking. I'm just trying to…get more of his attention."

Me: "Is it possible to take his hand?"

'X': "I have my arms around his shoulders."

Me: "Right. Good. You need to send as much love as possible to that person."

'X': "I'm trying to get him onto his feet now."

Me: "Try to get him to see that there is some hope. That although his life has been terrible, it does not necessarily have to continue like that. That there are people here waiting, and family waiting for him, but he needs to take a little step, he needs to look for the light, he needs to find that love and reassurance that is there for him."

'X': "There's somebody with her as well now, and they're going…crackers…trying to attract his attention."

'Z': "Which direction is he facing?"

'X': "Well he's standing up now, and he's facing this radiator, but they're over here."

'Z': "Well, then tell him that."

Me: "She's trying."

'X': "I am."

'Z': "And say to him.."

'X': "He's got his eyes shut."

'Z': "Well, tell him to open them."

'X': "There must be a great light there, as he's squinting and that, and shading his eyes now."

Me: "Good. Right, well tell him.."

'X': "Like blinding him now."

'Z': "Well, tell him to walk into it, and as he walks into it he will find someone there to collect him. Yeah?"

'X': "Yeah. They're with him now. There are three of them… they've got him. They've got him."
'Z': "Good, excellent!"
Me: "We thank them, and we also thank that person in the background, that helped us. Okay 'X'?"
'X': "Yeah."
Me: "Okay 'Y'?"
'Y': "Mmmmm."
Me: "Can you tell us something about this person now?"
'Y': "I feel she is quite an old lady, with a shawl round her shoulders."
[*A minute of silence followed*]
Me: "What is she doing?"
'Y': "She suddenly disappeared!"
'Z': "Changed her mind perhaps."
Me: "Maybe she's not sure."
'Z': "Or gone back for something."
Me: "She may come back – you never know."
'X': "Can you see anything around my throat?"
Me: "No. Why?"
'X': "I feel as if someone has got their hands round my throat."
Me: "Okay."
'X': "Or whether it's…"
Me: "You're fine! There are no hands round your throat, but… can you get an idea who it is? What sort of person it is?"
'X': "It's like someone put some kind of neck collar on me."
'Z': "You don't think it's the young man trying to put the collar round you?"
'X': "No."
'Z': "Then why, why have you got the condition of the collar then?"
'X': "I don't know."
Me: "Can you get any idea of this person?"
'X': "I can't see a person."
Me: "Right."
'Z': "Well tell them to take it off you immediately. Don't want any

condition like that. Tell them to take it off you right away. Has it gone?"

'X': "It's like a scarf."

Me: "It's a scarf not a collar?"

'X': "It's like a scarf."

Me: "Right. What colour is it?"

'X': "A creamy colour."

'Z': "So you got a lady with you. 'Y' what were you going to say there?"

'Y': "You're butting in!"

'Z': "Sorry."

'Y': "And where is your link? Somebody has just said that to me."

Me: "You're being told off 'Z'!"

'Z': "Aye, I got the lady."

Me: "Right. Try to link in."

'Y': "Somebody very…powerful."

Me; "Can you get anything yet 'X'?"

'X': "It's only at the front, there's nothing round the back or the sides. It's only at the front. I'm trying to think of it could be one of them muffler things. But it's bulking up…underneath the chin. And it feels soft and warm, but it's pushing my chin up. It's like it's though…if you can think of a big fur collar, you double up under your chin – it's like that."

Me: "Yes? I can't think of anything."

'X': "I feel as though my mouth could start dribbling."

'Z': "I know what it is. The woman is wearing a collar, one of those collars that holds the neck."

Me: "Right, a neck-brace?"

'Z': "Yeah. You know those white collars, that's what it is. I just sort of see her now, she couldn't speak. I can see her now. Her hair is white. But when she was here, there wasn't a hair out of place, she was immaculate. But something happened to her – the lights have gone funny [*the red lights changed in intensity*] – and it's to do with the neck."

Me: "'Y', have you got anything to add to that? [*No reply*] No? Okay. She had something wrong with her neck. So why is she here, is she here to help someone else, or is she here to meet someone?"

'Z': "She is looking for her husband. He went before she did and that's why she is looking for him. She's not here or there, she's sort of midway, sort of in-between."

Me: "So she hasn't moved on?"

'Z': "She's almost there, but she's not quite there. She's only been over for sixteen months."

Me: "Right. So she needs to then.."

'Z': "She's looking for her husband; can't get her name…"

Me: "Right. First we need to tell her that having passed over, that condition doesn't have to apply, and that if she wants to speak she could. And also, that there will be people there to help her, to guide her to the light. She needs to look towards the light, she needs to move on. This condition that she experienced on earth does not need to be experienced in spirit, and that as soon as she moves into the light, she will lose this condition, she will get help, she will get healing and she will find her loved ones. She needs reassurance now, that she can actually move on. We can try and ask one of her relatives, friends, or even her husband to try to attract her attention."

'Z': "A gentleman has just come in. It's her husband. He was a vicar. I can see him as plain as day. Quite a handsome looking man, glasses on. And his name is 'Bert' or 'Bertie'. He's saying that he wishes now that he could talk more about 'this'. He used to talk more in an orthodox way, a Christian way, but realises now that there is more to it. He's sorry… something happened between him and his wife, but I don't know what. He's coming for her. He's also thanking 'X', to keep up the good work."

Me: "Has she seen him yet?"

'X': "I can't do anything this minute, because I am that woman!"

'Me: "Well then turn towards the light."

[*'Z' spoke but his words were indistinct*]

Me: "That condition is there so you can link in – that is all. You don't have to have that condition at all. And you don't because *you* can speak!"

'Z': "Don't use 'X' like that! Leave…alone."

Me: "Just explain to her that, that condition is an earth condition, and that she no longer needs it. That her husband is there waiting for her. That all she needs to do is to turn to the light. Just reassure her, and help her to move that little bit towards the light. The person she is looking for is there waiting, but she has to make the first move. Nothing can be done unless she makes the first move. It's up to her. It is time to end this endless search – end! The person she is looking for is there waiting. Is she ready now to move?"

'X': "I'm just trying to get him to take a step forward, as he's just standing waiting."

Me: "But *she* needs to move. She needs to move. The light is there waiting for her, her husband is there waiting for her."

'X': "Yeah. She's seen him now."

Me: "Good."

'Z': "She's gone now."

'X': "Yeah."

Me: "Good. We send our love."

'X': "He's got his arm around her now. Oh! That was strange that!"

Me: "I bet it was. Take a drink of water 'X'."

'X': "I can tell you where she was. She was in an old folks home, sitting in a chair, and she had them carpet slippers on, like brown check, with them furry bobbles on the end. And she had her knees open and her skirt was above her knees, and she had these brown tights on. And sitting, she couldn't move. And this thing was around here, and all that was numb (indicating her chin and upper neck) and it was like as though she was dribbling, and her arms were even like that."

Me: "Right. Good. And how about you 'Y'?"

'Y': "Okay thank you."

Me: "Good. Well, it is just about time now.

The circle was closed shortly afterwards.

I made another list of notes for discussion next time.

1. *Bluebell and Matthew – why? Maybe indicating that we can call on them for help if need be.*
2. *Two came at the same time, on the mother vibration.*
3. *Many who have not passed into the light are 'looking for' family/loved ones.*
4. *Not all mothers/family etc., can come to help, hence that nurse that 'popped in' to escort the coalman to the light.*
5. *Old lady with shawl?*
6. *'Z' told off for butting in. My fault also.*
7. *'X' given condition but let herself 'become' that lady. MUST remain emotionally detached. If link that close ask them to speak through you. Also was asked to try to make lady move, instead she tried to get husband to move. Back to first principles: the POWER and WORLD of THOUGHT.* **This is a serious issue.**

20/12/07 First we sat for a discussion on the notes from the last meeting. We came to no firm conclusion on number 1. On 2 we agreed that getting double links would probably speed up things, and had nothing really to add for 3 or 4. On number 5 we thought that some may come but change their minds at the last minute. Many of these people are 'on the verge', and may pass over anyway when they see the others go through to the light. On number 6 'Z' said he would hold back, so I will have to try to pick up some of what 'Z' would normally give out. The longest discussion was on number 7; but we all agreed that we had to be in control, we had to be that one step back, mentally and emotionally, so that we could help anybody. We had to be like paramedics – ready to face any situation. I said that I would do a little 'training' exercise sometime in the new year, as it would be necessary if we are to continue and go deeper into this line of work.

Then the main lights were switched off and the red lights put on. After opening the circle, we opened it to those not yet passed over.

Within a minute, I asked 'X' if anybody was with her. She said that she had a young woman, late 30s/early 40s, who was very distraught and confused, and was pacing up and down. 'X' thought that she had committed suicide at this time of year, it was all the stress, anxiety and wondering where her next bit of money would come from, she had been trying to cope but couldn't.

I then asked 'Z' if he could link into that. He said he was aware of the lady, but that he had a different link. He was aware of a male and female between 'Y' and himself. The man was known as 'Woody' as his name was Alan. He had spectacles on, was in his 30s/40s, had a slim build and looked a bit like the actor as well. He went quickly and 'Z' thought it was suicide as well. He also had this Maori or Hawaiian character – this was a memory of a holiday, he was due to get married and his 'bride' let him down very badly. Quickly I went to 'Y' but she had no link.

So I went back to 'X', who said that her woman had calmed down a bit. The woman's fingers were nicotine stained and she had a tattoo on her arm, she had a cleaning job, but also a rough life. 'X' thought by the clothes that the woman was wearing that she may have passed in the 1980s or earlier, that she was talking about green shield stamps and that her name was Pamela. Then I talked a bit about moving on, about going towards the light. 'X' said the woman was apprehensive due to what she had done (suicide). I tried to reassure her on that, and then left 'X' to talk to her mentally. After a minute or two 'X' said she was ready now, and within a minute she had gone through to the light.

Then I turned to 'Z', who said that his person had headed towards the light. [*We thought later that the female energy that 'Z' had picked up at the start was probably the one that had brought him.*]

So we opened out again and within a couple of minutes 'Z' said he had somebody called 'George', who had been in limbo since 1978/79. He was a bit of a daredevil and into motorbikes and that is what had taken him to spirit. He had big sideburns and shoulder length greasy hair. He had never believed in any of this and was a bit sceptical, set in his ways. He saw the door and some mates came to welcome him and took him into the light.

'X' then reported that she had a big burley bald headed man, sitting in an ox blood coloured leather armchair, in front of the fire. He was a docker, hard man, who had made his wife's life miserable. He was now crying like a baby in repentance. He probably passed over in the 1950s, and his wife's name was Mary. I suggested to 'X' that she try to get him to his feet, but he was a bit reluctant at first. Then 'X' mentioned that he had a little girl who had died. 'Z' then indicated that the girl was there. I told him to put his hand out and that his child would clasp it and bring him through to the light. Shortly after, 'X' said that he had been taken through.

After asking 'Y' if she had anybody – but hadn't – I said we had time for another, so we opened out again. Within twenty seconds 'X' said she had a little boy in a field all by himself, but he didn't seem to have a care in the world. His name was 'Martin', aged about nine, and he was looking for his friends. I talked for a bit and then asked 'X' how he was doing. She remarked that he was a little hyperactive, that he thought his friends were hiding in the cornfield and he was looking for them. He was thinking that 'X' was trying to trick him, to get him in for bed! I then asked 'Z' to comment. He told 'X' to get the boy out of the cornfield first, to go to the edge of the field. 'X' replied that he couldn't take that angle. 'X' was trying to befriend him at the moment, so I gave her some time, but also expressed a wish for Bluebell. 'Z' then said that Bluebell was there. 'X' remarked that she was walking with him to the corner; now he could see somebody, but then wished it were a boy not a girl! Then in a few moments Bluebell had taken him through to the light.

Then all came back to normal awareness. At this point I lit a tealight and put it into a star patterned holder, and then we linked hands around the circle. "As we come to the end of this year, we would like – as a circle – to thank all our helpers, all those behind the scenes who have worked so hard on our behalf, so that we may actually start doing some work. We thank them for their perseverance and their love and their encouragement. And we thank all those individual guides, and teachers, and helpers and friends, who have helped us throughout the year, who may sometimes have to face disappointment and bewilderment at some of our actions, but hopefully we may tread a straighter path, a truer path next year. We would like to thank them greatly for their help as we come to close this circle, and hopefully in two weeks, when we start again, we will go forward in the new year with renewed vigour, a little bit more wisdom, and hopefully more love – a bigger heart." We then ended and had a brief discussion. All commented on the coldness they had experienced and 'Z' felt that 'Y' had given out a lot this evening, to which 'Y' concurred.

10/01/08 We talked briefly at the start about the last meeting. I said that I wouldn't go round everybody as usual, but would go with the first person and others could chip in if they were linked. Otherwise, they should hold their own link and if able send them to the light themselves, as 'Z' was able to do last time. This was agreed.

It took several minutes after we had opened up, before anyone spoke. 'Z' said that he saw a little black dog. 'X' then said she had the impression of a well or shaft, that was very cold, dark and deep, but there was a, "heck of a commotion at the top of it". It seemed that there was a crowd of people trying to get somebody up from the shaft/well, and that dog belonged to a male person who was down the shaft. There were two wooden doors/covers at the top of the shaft, and the crouching figure at the bottom was a young boy of about 14/15. I asked 'Y' if she could add anything and she said she had the idea that it was around the 1920s, this due to the style of clothing that she saw on the schoolchildren running across the playground. She had the impression that this was a sudden disaster – like Aberfan. I then asked 'X' if she had anything further. She mentioned that the boy had clogs on his feet, that were crumpled under him, and that his name was 'Peter'. I asked 'X' to first reassure him, telling him that we had come to help him, and then try to get him to stand up. 'X' then said that she was confused as to whether the light at the top of the shaft was spirit or not, as it had started in daylight. Then I asked 'X' again to first try to get him to his feet. I then also tried to encourage him. Next 'X' had him on his feet and with a bit of encouragement he was rising up the shaft to the light. Then 'X' said that Peter was with his dog and 'through', but for the first time someone had gone to the light in the direction of between 'Y' and myself, instead of between 'X' and 'Z'.

There was a pause for a couple of minutes before 'Z' said he saw a billy goat, and while he was watching it he got a pain down his left side, right down his arm and leg. Then he got an elderly man named 'Joe', who said he had come for his goat. Joe had a pipe and a flat cap, and was sad. He wanted to help someone but they were not coming forward, and it was to do with family. It appears that there had been a big falling out, and he wanted to make it up. However, 'Z' didn't know where the other person was. I said I didn't quite get where the goat fitted in and asked if anybody else could give anything on it. 'Y' then said, "Ask the goat who it represents". Then 'Z' said 'Billy' was Joe's brother. Billy wouldn't speak to us. The rift in the family was over money; Billy was rumbled by Joe and didn't like it. 'Z' then declared that he saw a peacock! A bit later 'Z' related that Joe had given Billy a candle and the latter was mellowing. Then there was a bit of confusion when Billy said, "that lady knows me", which we thought referred to 'Y'. But in actual fact referred to a lady 'Y' was linked with. It transpired that the lady was his mother and a schoolteacher. Then 'Z' said that Billy was standing by the door and that he entered the light with his mother following him.

After a few minutes 'Z' heard voices singing 'Amazing Grace'. 'X' then announced she had a chapel or gospel hall, however, she didn't see any people, just the wooden floor and dusty furniture, and that it smelled musty. After a bit 'Z' reported it was a lady who was playing the organ (which 'X' picked up first), but she was heart-broken having been badly let down, and she hadn't come to terms with what had happened. Her happiest memories were playing and singing; she wanted to see her mother but didn't want to see 'him'. Next 'Z' saw horses; she had a great love of horses. Shortly after that 'Z' managed to get her to the light, reunited with her mother. Then she turned round and said, "thank you" to 'X'. I thanked the mother and all those animals that had come to help.

Then I brought them back to normal awareness. 'X' closed the circle.

17/01/08 At first we talked about the last meeting. It transpired that the lady that 'Y' had, the schoolteacher and mother of 'Billy' (the second one), had been with her the whole time, even during the first one – that is why she said the 1920s. Then we talked about the third one. 'X' said it had been a mission hall and 'Y' immediately commented that it was connected to the Salvation Army. She also reminded us that the 11th had been the anniversary of the passing of a mutual friend of ours, and she had Salvation Army connections, and also had played the organ!

Then we changed the lights and opened up in prayer. I asked the circle members to just speak when they had somebody with them. After a couple of minutes 'Z' looked like he had somebody, so I asked him. He replied that it was a little unclear at present, but he had a gentleman behind him. A little later 'Z' announced that he was hearing, "help me, help me." The person had gone over very quickly and that a car was involved, but 'Z' could not actually see him. 'Z' next mentioned that the person had been thrown out of his body very quickly, and that he was very agitated and saying, "their fault, their fault." Asking 'X' if she could link to this she said that she had somebody else, so I told her to hold on to that person.

Asking 'Y', she declared that all she got was 'black ice' and that it happened recently, that it happened on a bend, but she also couldn't see him.

After about ten minutes we still hadn't got much further except that the person was very young, and that 'Z' was picking up a lot of pain. I then said that we needed a little help from 'our' angels. After sixteen minutes 'Z' reported that he saw the light now, but he could not yet see him but was aware that somebody else had come in. 'Y' stated that she had seen a doctor come in with a bag and a white coat on, and then a nurse; he needed a lot of help, as he didn't understand about the other side of life. 'Z' mentioned that he got a foreign connection with the person, and 'Y' said he needed to be taken to the light and then to the Halls of Healing. 'X' then suggested that as he was young he could 'go over the bridge'. Then 'Z' reported that he had lost him altogether. 'Y' said that the doctor and nurse took him, but that he was still in the dark. With things getting confused, 'X' then announced that somebody had jumped on her and was clinging to her, but being so small the rest of us said that she had somebody else. 'Z' remarked that he thought that the man was Polish and didn't understand us due to the language. Next 'Y' noted that somebody who knew his language was with him and was holding his hand. Finally, after some twenty-five minutes, 'Y' reported that he had been taken into the light.

When we turned to 'X', she mentioned that she had a different person earlier, but now she had this little boy who was clinging, with his arms and legs wrapped round her. He was wearing rough shorts and had grubby knees, with socks half up and half down, a knitted cardigan, and was about 7 or 8 years old. 'X' thought that his name was 'Bobby'. She said his face was all grubby and tear-stained and he was looking for his twin brother 'Billy'. 'Z' said his brother was in spirit, to which 'X' replied, "he will be now", as it was quite a while ago. So I asked Billy to come and guide Bobby to the light. Next 'X' observed a family waving, silhouetted by the light, and then Bobby was running towards them and was over!

I then asked 'X' about the first person that she had got. She declared that it was in a foreign country and she had seen a young lad with long hair, he was clean but naked except for a bit of cloth around him. She thought it was white sand that 'they' were pulling him out of, but his hands were above his head – bound, and his feet were down. For ages he would not open his eyes but eventually did, and finally rose to the light in the position he had been in; as 'X' said, "a bit like Superman".

After several minutes 'Z' mentioned that he was in a bedroom and that there was a girl crying. The room was dark and dismal and the girl had been ill-treated. She knew that she needed to look for the light, and was asking for help as to where it was. However, she was saying that she didn't want to forgive. 'Z' thought she was a teenager of about 13 or 14, abused by her father or step-father and her mother was helpless in a roundabout way, but wasn't a part of it. 'Z' thought it was some time ago, maybe about forty years. She had short straight blond hair with a round face, a blouse and cardigan on, a skirt and white socks and slip on shoes, and was sitting on the edge of the bed. Her name was Clare. Her mother had now passed over, but the person who was coming for her was somebody else, in some sort of uniform, like a nurse, and then took her to the light. Just at the end 'Z' announced that she was Welsh.

I then asked 'Y', who commented that she had a real old grandmother with her. 'Z' linked in and declared that she was there to help. 'Y' then said that there was a very little girl, and that when she goes the grandmother will go with her. A bit later 'Y' reported that they had both gone over. [*At that point the lights changed.*]

I brought the circle back to normal awareness and 'Y' closed the circle. We had a short discussion. 'X' reported that as soon as 'Y' got up to say the closing prayer the lights had gone up also. Then 'Y' explained that the grandmother had come to stand by the child until she died, and that they then both went to the light together. 'Z' mentioned that the young Polish man was so agitated that he couldn't understand us speaking English.

24/01/08 We started with discussing other points from the last circle. 'Y' had said to me before we had gone to the room that she wasn't happy, and she brought up the fact that the first person had come through 'Z' and that he therefore should have finished it off – but he had lost him and 'Y' had to get him to the light. I then brought up that as 'Z' had been picking up that the young man was in pain, I should have asked for a doctor/nurse to come in to help him, as I presumed we had a 'medical team' with us behind the scenes. 'Y' then said that she was puzzled as to when she should come in or stay out! So I went over our *agreed* policy again, and 'X' backed that up.

'Y' then said that dangers could come in with this, that something could come through and attach themselves to one of us, and she wouldn't be able to cope with that. Also she was puzzled about the grandmother who had come for the little girl, and I said that it was a puzzle to me too.

'Z' had been silent for some time and had been asking questions in his mind; he now said, "permission to speak?" I replied in the affirmative and he then related that he had been quietly trying to tune in. He said that all he kept getting was that we are a team, for this purpose. He had asked if he had lost that man and the answer to that was, *"no you didn't"*, that none of us had lost anything. Asking why, the swift reply came, *"because you have to remember that in this type of work there will be all sorts of condition and reasons for, with each individual soul; hence the demands that meet this type of work. But fear not, you are correct that there are those who are behind the scenes with you. They will not fail you. We do expect little errors, but you can learn from that. For we would not allow or let in those who we did not think, for one moment, that you are not capable of dealing with. So the answer is that each one of us here, you have to remember that there will be those who will be in need or 'in extremis'. In other words, known as the astral plane, and it is there that it can become a little difficult for that person alone, for their souls to see the actual light themselves. So a little extra help will encourage them in need. This is where the strength and knowledge comes in, not only from the sitters but from those who are dealing with it from the other side too. This is where you have to work together as a team, to show the individual soul where he or she is to go. Just remember, the light is that way. Send them in that direction towards that light, the light is there, it is not anywhere else.* [A couple of words that were inaudible followed.] *It was there for you in the beginning, that is where it is. As for linking in, linking in can come with your own, but also if you are with whomever you are with, then that is where the extra help is coming in. So do not think for one moment that anyone is doing more or less, or regardless or whatever. The important issue is that you are with who you are, in order to help the individual soul or souls, to be shown the way to the light. That some will be a little bit more difficult than others, it is simply because there are those who will be in limbo. That young man, he was thrown dramatically out of his body, he did not know where he was or what had actually happened to him. He stayed in that limbo state until he saw the glimmer of light here, which is why it was slightly difficult to reach him. But, the important thing is, you got him there – and that's what matters! Thank you for listening."*

As we had been some time since the start of the circle, I said that we could come back to any of this later, but that we had work to do. The ordinary light was turned off and the red lights put on. We opened out, and I asked them to speak as soon as they had somebody with them.

Within a minute 'X' said that she had a soldier with her who had a rough brown uniform, with a rough felt belt. He had his back to her and was very, very agitated. He was looking at his watch as he was to meet somebody at twelve o'clock, and he wasn't where he should be, and the other person wasn't there. He had passed over in action, but his body wasn't damaged. I asked 'X' to try to turn him around. Then I asked if any of the others could relate to this, but nobody answered. A bit later 'X' asked if he could be given an order, as he was a military man. Apparently his name was 'David' and he had now turned around. I asked if maybe a friend or superior officer could come to help. 'X' then reported that he was really standing to attention now, and that he was being marched off into the light.

A few minutes later 'Z' said that he had been asking quietly about things, and had been shown different people who were with us. Between him and 'X' stood an Arab type figure with a big sword in front of the door; he was in charge. He had a magnificent blue stone in his headwear. Next he saw 'Y's matron, the nursing type standing between him and 'Y', as was an American Indian with full headdress. Standing near 'X' was a beautiful smiling Indian princess type, with rich, luxurious dark hair and pretty leggings. Then an Arab on a camel came in. He got off the camel and stood near me; he had white robes on and a black band round his head. Then between 'Y' and myself were a nurse and a doctor. The doctor had wise-looking features, white silvery hair and gold spectacles and was very gentle. The nurse looked in her late 30s or early 40s, very pleasant looking. Then 'Z' said that at that point somebody came in who needed help, he had hanged himself. His name was 'Joe' and he was a farmer. 'Z' could see his lifeless body hanging from a tree. He was remorseful, and realised it was wrong, and knew he had to go to the light, but was a bit unsure how his family would react. But with 'Z's encouragement he went into the light.

Within a minute 'Z' had made another link, and asked, "who is Mrs. Clark?" It would seem that the person was helping 'Y'. This person was straight laced and strict.

Next I asked 'X' if she had anybody, and she replied that she had a man who was crouching down that had been mauled by an animal. At first she wasn't sure if it was in the wild or in a zoo or circus. It transpired later that it was probably the last of these. The man was in his early 50s, his hair was thinning on top and was curly and dirty, and he had an open-necked red shirt on. 'X' said he was terror-struck, frozen to the spot. So I asked if the doctor could step in and help. Within a short time 'Z' noted that he saw the doctor going in. 'X' then asked if he was getting an injection, and 'Y' confirmed it. I asked if he could get up, but 'X' said that she thought that the injection had sedated him. Next 'Z' announced that the man was being carried into the light by the doctor and nurse, which was again confirmed by 'Y'.

Within a minute 'Z' stated that he had someone who passed because of their heart. He was sitting in a chair at home and he passed very quickly. Slightly overweight, maybe late 40s/early 50s, he had several health problems, diabetes etc. He was a bit of a loner and had never really thought about death or the afterlife. A bit timid, he saw the light, but was a bit unsure of what he would find! However, the nurse came and took him by the hand and led him into the light.

'Z' said that he saw somebody sitting over there (behind me somewhere) but would tell us about it later. As nobody had a link, I brought them back to normal awareness. 'Z' then closed the circle.

When I asked if there was anything about tonight that they wished to discuss, 'Z' said that what he had seen was remarkable in its clarity (regarding circle helpers in spirit), and that he had seen Matthew sitting watching intently.

31/01/08 We sat under red light, turned up at the start, and discussed a few points from last time. I said that we had been given reassurance as well as an idea of some of the spirits who are working with us. 'Z' emphasised the clarity with which he saw spirit. I also mentioned that spirit had used the words 'in extremis', and that in my dictionary it had two meanings: (1) In an extremely difficult situation; (2) At the point of death. I thought that the second meaning may go some way to explain why we had the grandmother coming for the dying child. Lastly, I briefly went over again about our policy on linking in.

We turned down the red lights and I said the opening prayer, before we invited those needing help to come to us. There were a couple of loud 'knocks' a minute or so before the first link. They seemed to come from behind 'X' and around the area where the pictures were. 'Z' got the first link: a man called 'Bernard' who was ready to move forward. He was looking for his wife, but was a bit confused. He didn't have any condition now, but in life he had Alzheimer's disease, and so mentally hadn't passed over properly at the time. Very quickly he saw the light and saying, "thank you" to us he went into it to meet his wife who was there.

After a minute or so, I suspected 'X' had somebody with her, so I asked. She stated she got the name 'Deakin' but could not see anybody at present. Then 'X' got an impression of an elderly, stoutish lady, who had fallen in some sort of passageway and that there were others around her helping. After about five minutes, 'Z' said that the lady was in a home. She fell down stairs in a cellar, and though others came to help it was too late. Later 'Z' clarified that she had gone down to get some coal. 'X' noted that the man climbing down had ropes on his back, so maybe they were needed to lift her out of the cellar. Eventually, after eighteen minutes, she was seen going into the light, with the others following behind her.

Then I asked 'Y' about the person she was linked with. 'Y' replied that she had a man who had passed with a heart attack; she could feel the pain down her left side. He hadn't wanted to go as he had things that he wanted to do, but in the end had thrown in the towel. 'Y' had reassured him that he could do many things from the light that he couldn't do on earth. He then went very quickly over to the light.

Within thirty seconds 'Y' got a link with potholers, with the lamps shining on their helmets. There was one man and two women, who had got caught by rising water (*the lights changed at this point*). Shortly they saw a person with a brighter light, and followed that person to get 'on land'. Then shortly after that they were taken to the light. After that 'Y' seemed to be consoling those friends 'on land' that everything was okay. I thought this odd but didn't pursue it at the time.

Next 'Z' got two names, 'Frank' and 'James', and a young man that said, "I didn't mean to do it". It transpired that he had hung himself, and that his name was Frank James. The doctor and nurse came to attend to him, with the nurse taking him by the arm to the light, and there he would be getting some healing.

While we were sitting in silence the lights changed again, and shortly 'Z' said that just before the change in the lights, he had got this flower – an orchid – from the mountainside as a reward, a pure white with a hint of pink or lilac with it, for all of us with every love and blessing.

A little later, as time was getting near the end of the circle, I asked each in turn if they had anybody – they said no. However, 'Y' replied that the only way she could describe it was that she felt like a Buddha, a healing Buddha. The lights changed as 'Z' asked if that is where the flower had come from, but 'Y' didn't know. I then brought them back to normal awareness. 'X' closed the circle.

In the discussion afterwards 'X' asked about the two noises that had occurred shortly after we had started. I said that I had heard them and that there were definitely two, and I would check on the recordings. 'X' thought they had occurred about 8.10pm. [*On listening to the recordings several days later, it was on the digital recorder but not very clear. However, on the tape recorder it came out clearly as two bangs – or more like 'slaps', which occurred roughly a minute before the first link.*] Also 'Y' said that her hands felt 'on fire' when the Buddha was there, and that she had felt like 'it' was going to speak.

7/02/08 We sat under red lights. I gave the opening prayer and then went through the usual sequence. Me: "And now, as we are linked hearts and minds, we ask that we may be linked to spirit, and start our preparation for the greater work to come, for the harder work that is to come. We invite you now to link to spirit." I mentally asked spirit to link with the three others so that I could perform the exercise that I had planned.

After a couple of minutes, I suddenly said, "Right! Come back to normal awareness!" And after a few seconds, "Back to normal awareness and open your eyes." 'Z' came back immediately, 'X' closely followed, but 'Y' was the last to make it, taking about twenty to twenty five seconds. I then apologized, but reminded them that they had been warned that I would do this at some point. 'X' asked what it was for, so I told her that it was important that they could follow my instructions, as there may be times ahead when there could be difficulties and they must be able to respond immediately on my command. I also told them that new circumstances might require that the whole power of the circle may be needed to help a particular person over. 'Y' at that point announced that she had just got, "have you all charged your batteries?" I then said that as soon as one had a link, to say that as soon as possible, so that everybody can link in immediately. Everybody seemed to agree to this. Then, having finished our exercise, we started again!

After nearly four minutes, 'Z' said that he saw a man, who reminded him of 'John Peel', wearing top hat, overcoat and waistcoat, from the Victorian era. 'Z' reported that the man said, "You're from Langwave (?), any chance of helping some of the people there?" 'Z' replied, "what do you mean?" Then the man showed what 'Z' took to be the astral plane, a tunnel that was very foggy. There were people wandering about, hardened souls, tramps and people like that. The man asked if he could help them, to which 'Z' stated that he would discuss it with the group first. The man said that he would get back to him. So I told 'Z' that if he saw him again, he should tell him that we would try. 'Z' then got a warning that some of them would be 'ragamuffins'.

Almost immediately after the above, 'Z' said that he saw three people, one a young lad and the other two slightly older. They were lost and had apparently drowned. Very quickly they saw the light and went over into it.

A couple of minutes later, 'Z' stated that a Native American in full headdress was standing in the corner, between 'X' and myself. He was just watching, having his arms folded and carrying a peace pipe. 'Z' got the name 'Grey Eagle', a tall but well built man who had died in battle, he seemed to be offering 'peace'.

After some minutes 'Z' asked 'X' if she had anyone, and when she said no he then asked 'Y'. She replied that she had a person but that he had gone, and she couldn't make head nor tail of it. When asked in what way, 'Y' said that the person had been in a wheelchair, his name was 'Joe' and he had part of one leg removed, and he didn't like to answer any questions about it. He had seen the light and had come down this dark tunnel to the light, and then seemed to be totally bewildered – and then she lost him. I said that he might come back. Three minutes passed before 'Y' announced that she had a war situation, and Joe had gone to bring back some of his mates; she said she had three or four soldiers. When I asked 'X', she replied that she had seen the Eiffel Tower horizontally, then she saw a man in the trenches, stubble on his chin and just shaking with fear. 'Y' then announced that they were aware of our light. I said they needed to move forward and if they looked carefully they may actually see a glimmer of the light. I asked 'Y' how they were responding, but got no answer. Then half a minute later 'Y' disclosed that they were now marching into the light. 'Z' confirmed this and said that the nurse was there attending to them.

It was nearly ten minutes later before 'Z' reported that he had a gentleman, who was a mountain climber, still climbing the mountains as he had not yet come to terms with having died. 'Z' said that the man was aware of him. I asked if he didn't fancy some new challenges, and if he climbed into the light he would like it. Next 'Z' said that somebody else, who he couldn't see properly, was leading the climber into the light.

With that, we thanked all those who had come to help, and those behind the scenes. 'X' closed the circle. During the discussion afterwards, 'Y' said she wouldn't be here next week, and I said that I wouldn't be here the week after that, as I had a Parent' Evening at school. I asked them if they had somebody with them when I did my little exercise at the beginning. 'X' said she just had 'drifty things' coming and going; 'Z' confirmed that he did, and 'Y' said no, but was just getting nicely connected. I said then that I had been a little early! I told 'Z' that it was interesting that he got that character from that long ago. 'Z' commented that he was sure the person was genuine and may indeed get back to us. Then I remarked that Grey Eagle was probably there to help us and later our contacts, when he appeared before we got connected to the soldiers, giving out peace.

21/02/08 'Y' was away on holiday. We sat under red lights that were turned up quite bright. I opened in prayer. Then I went over the 'rules' again: to say as soon as possible if you think you have a link, so that the others can link in at once, thereby all of us working as a team. We are getting to a different level and need to work together more. 'X' said she was reluctant to speak out, but hopefully understood my reasoning. 'Z' backed me up and told 'X' that she needs to ask more, in time she will know instinctively if she has got a contact or not. Then I mentioned that I wouldn't be here next week, and that I was putting 'X' in charge. 'X' laughed, but it will be good experience for her.

Then we went through our usual sequence and turned the red lights lower. After a couple of minutes the lights dimmed, so I asked 'X' if she had anybody. She replied, "no", and so I asked 'Z'. at first there was no response, so I asked again, and then he replied that he was aware of the Indian chief Grey Eagle standing in the corner again. 'Z' thought that he would speak to us when he is ready.

A couple of minutes later 'Z' reported that he had a gentleman whose name was 'George'; he was a Christian – but not a very good one. 'Z' asked him what he was doing, and it appeared that he was looking for 'Isobel' – his mother. Very quickly, he went towards the light and was met by his mother, who told 'Z' that George hadn't been bad at all, that it was just his way of thinking.

Another couple of minutes and 'Z' reported that he was icy cold on his left side, and that he thought somebody from spirit was occupying 'Y's chair. 'Z' couldn't make out who or even what sex this person was.

Shortly after that the lights changed again, and soon 'Z' reported that he had a young man, his name was 'Duncan', who had died in a car crash. 'Z' said he had known of him, but that he now wants to move on. He had been in the gym business, body building etc., and had been a rugby player. He was making his way to the light and his granddad came to greet him, and the young man said, "nice one" as he moved into the light.

About eight minutes later the lights went again, and I asked 'X' first, and when I got a negative reply, asked 'Z' if he had anybody. He announced that he thought that there was a Chinaman sitting in 'Y's seat. I suggested it might be 'Y's Chinaman, but 'Z' said he thought it might be Ho-Lin; he was watching and recording things. 'Z' was getting a very humble and gentle feeling with him. 'Z' stated that he asked if it was Ho-Lin and got the reply, "don't ask silly question!"

Four or five minutes later 'Z' announced that he was in a house with a young man. The young man had hanged himself over his girlfriend and other things; he was really stuck and couldn't move on, with a lot of anger as well as anguish. His mind kept going back to the house. 'Z' was trying to pacify him. I asked 'Z' if he thought that the young man might need the attention of the doctor. Within a minute both doctor and nurse were reported to be there, but the man was still stubborn. Then 'Z' reported that the man's dog had come in, and the man had picked it up, and was mellowing a bit. Spirit told 'Z', "we have ways and means you know." During all this time the lights were changing frequently. Soon the doctor and nurse took the young man, with his dog, into the light.

Even after that, the lights kept changing every now and then. It happened so frequently that I asked 'Z' to relax, as I thought that maybe spirit was going to speak to us through him. However, nothing came of it, despite the lights still changing. I brought them back to normal awareness and then 'Z' closed the circle.

28/02/08 I was absent.

6/03/08 At the start we went over the general policy again. Everybody seemed satisfied with this. The red lights were turned down and we opened as usual. Nothing happened for quite some time, though the lights changed slightly several times, and I was wondering if anybody would speak. I had decided that I was not going to ask them directly!

Some seventeen minutes later, 'Z' reported that he had a young man who had been killed in a motorbike accident. The young man had not yet got the gist of what was happening and kept going back to where he was buried. The bike was a wreck; he came in contact with a lorry on a bend and went over very quickly. At this point 'Y' came in and asked 'Z' if the young man was called 'Joe', and 'Z' confirmed that. She said that she had a woman called 'Mary Ellen' with her for ages, and this woman was looking for Joe. 'Y' observed that the bike was old, from the 1920s. Then 'Y' stated that when I had been speaking [*In the preparation period.*], it was as if I was a priest taking a funeral service, and then there was this woman standing. Next, all of a sudden, the coffin was in the ground and the people were in black standing on the other side. 'Y' had not been able to work it out, but had got the name Mary Ellen, who was looking for Joe. I said that I thought Joe was ready now to go over, and 'Z' reported that a woman had taken Joe by the arm towards the light. Within a very short time Joe had gone over.

A few minutes later the red lights went down and then up again. 'Z' spoke soon after that, saying that he had a miner who was looking for his mates. 'Z' saw several men with their lights on in their helmets. He felt that the man had passed when there was a cave-in. 'Z' was then badly affected by picking up the conditions from the miner: in great pain round his stomach and ribs area. I suggested we send in the doctor and nurse to attend to the miner. After a minute or so, somebody took the miner back a bit away from 'Z', who felt better as a consequence. 'Z' got the other miners together, about eight to ten of them, and asked them to go to the light, which they did including the original miner.

Again, before the next contact the lights flashed. 'Z' saw a little girl holding someone's hand, he thought her mother, and they were looking for the wee girl's brother. 'Z' thought it was going back a long time by the clothes they were wearing. These two had passed and were going to the cemetery but couldn't find anything. 'Z' felt that the boy was called 'James or Jamie'. 'Y' then announced that there had been an outbreak of diphtheria and the little boy had been left in hospital. The little girl and her mother had died before the boy, so he was still 'there'. I asked if Bluebell could help us, at which point the lights flashed. Next 'Z' reported that the nurse was there, and the little girl got the boy by giving him his teddy, and then they all went into the light very happy.

I then brought them back to normal awareness in the room. I asked 'Y' when she had actually got Mary Ellen. When she replied that it was when I was talking, I reminded her that she should have said about it. We then discussed various 'bits' of the circle. 'X' said that she didn't get anybody, just had various faces and 'circumstances'. She then closed the circle.

13/03/08 Sitting under the red lights, I opened in prayer. Then told the group that there was nothing really to report from last week, just reminded them to give out as soon as they had something, so that the rest could link in. Did the usual sequence after that.

After about three and a half minutes the lights changed and a few seconds later 'Z' reported that he had a gentleman with him, who took his own life. He hung himself, but was now ready to pass over. He was full of remorse at what he had done, as he now knew it was not the answer. Within a very short time 'Z' said that his grandmother had come and took the man by the hand and led him into the light.

At the start of the circle I had been wondering if somebody was working with 'X' 'behind the scenes', and the thought came into my head that it might be a Native American girl; I asked if this was so and looked at the lights, but there was no change. As I usually do, I regularly looked around the room, and noticed that the lights reflected in the picture of the Native American woman, which hung on the wall behind 'X', were moving. After checking this **very** closely and regularly during the circle, I was certain that the picture was moving, or at least its surface was! This happened continually during the circle.

After several minutes the lights changed downwards and a little later went back up again. 'Z' then said that somebody was standing between 'Y' and myself. After a long silence, I asked 'Z' if this was somebody from spirit, which he confirmed. He wasn't sure if it was a man or a woman, but thought the latter.

A little later 'Z' said he had a woman with him – at that point the lights flickered. She was quite upset and wanted her children. 'Z' saw a backyard with washing hanging out, he thought it went back to the 1940s or 50s. The house had caught fire because she had left the chip pan on and she had never got over losing her very young children. The children were in spirit, but she had not moved on because of her mental anguish. 'Z' reported that he detected two children at the doorway to the light. He also heard someone saying that she was not to blame. Within a very short time she was through into the light.

After about ten minutes the red lights flickered and again approximately three minutes after that. [*Between these two events, two knocks were heard on the tape recording, then one knock, and again another knock – this was not picked up on the digital recording.*] Twenty or so seconds later 'Z', who had been looking intently at 'X', asked her who was with her, to which she replied that she had nobody.

[*There was a sound on the tape recording for a few brief seconds of what sounded like interference from a mobile phone – again this was not picked up on the digital recording. A minute or so after that were another two knocks, could be feet moving, maybe 'Z's feet hitting the legs of his chair; again this was not picked up on the digital recording.*]

Not long after this 'Z' announced that he had an airman from the Second World War. His uniform was light blue, RAF, and he was the pilot and that there were four others. The captain was asking his crew if they would go with him to the light. 'Z' thought it was 1943 and in a foreign country, maybe France, the plane came down in fog and all were killed. 'Z' reported that the nurse came in and within a minute had brought them back into the light. He also got thanks from Captain 'Bradley' or 'Bradbury'.

Coming back to normal awareness, we gave thanks to those who had come to help and to those behind the scenes. We then had a short discussion. I asked 'Z' that when he asked 'X' if she had anybody, did he see anybody? When he affirmed this I asked who he had seen and he replied that it was a Native American. When I suggested that it was a woman he confirmed this. At that point I then told them that the picture behind 'X' had been moving all night, and that I thought that the Native American woman was working with and 'on' 'X'. 'X' then said that she got absolutely nothing, not even a flicker! 'X' then asked 'Y' if she had got anything. 'Y' said that she had no legs on her, from the knees down. Then she said that she had people at the start, but that she said 'go' as she didn't want them. There had been a policeman with a girl in ankle chains, but the language from her had been 'terrible', and that she wouldn't calm down.

I said the energy seemed to change quite a bit tonight. When 'Z' asked about the lights, I reported that they had changed at least six times during the circle, usually before somebody came through.

20/03/08 We went down a little early to discuss some points from last week. I told them that the picture behind 'X' had definitely been moving, as I had checked it carefully several times during the circle; it had been moving in two different directions – sideways and up and down. Also related about the knocks on the tape and that I thought that they had come from low down, and had assumed that it was 'Z's feet hitting his chair legs. However 'Z' didn't think he had done that and 'X' didn't remember anything like that happening, and I had to confess that I had not picked it up at the time. I said that it had happened at least four or five times and was on the tape, but not on the digital recording. Then I told them about the 'jingle' from the mobile phone being on the tape for about a second, but again it was not on the digital recording. 'Z' reminded us that spirit would often build up energy, psychic rods, etc., from low down under the table, but it would often rise as the power and energy increased, but that spirit are capable of anything!

Next I ran through things about the 'new policy'; the information from spirit was that we were to experience 'harder cases' from the astral plane, so we were to 'be prepared', so that is why we all had to link together as one. I reminded 'Y' that she should have told us that she had got that woman with the policeman, and that it was the second time in a row that she hadn't spoken out! 'Y' acknowledged that she should have said something – but I didn't get a categorical assurance that she would stick fully to the policy!

After saying the opening prayer, we went through our usual sequence and turned the red lights down low. As soon as I had settled myself and checked the others, I noticed that the picture was moving again and continued to do so – every time that I looked – until the end of the circle. After three and a half minutes the lights flickered and about three minutes after that 'Z' reported that he had a gentleman with him. He was called 'Len' or 'Lenny', a 'well made' man who had been in this situation for some time. He had a wife waiting for him. He was very overweight and had lots of health problems in life, and hadn't thought much about the situation after death. [*The lights went up and down a few times during all this and a few times before the end.*] His wife was called 'Edna' and she was waiting for him; it was the anniversary date of their wedding. Very shortly he went into the light with his wife.

Four minutes later the lights went again and immediately 'Y' stated that she had a boy, aged about thirteen, who had been 'showing off' on his bicycle. Going round and round a playground and then suddenly he had gone into a wall, receiving a head injury that killed him. His name is 'Brian', but he is concerned that his brother and sister would see him with his disfigurement. 'Y' asked him if there was anyone he would like to see, and he said his great uncle. So we asked if he would come, or alternatively maybe a nurse. Within a short space of time he went to his great uncle in the light, taking his bag and bike with him.

Within four and a half minutes 'Z' said that he had a young man and behind him he could see a house burning. [*Again the lights flashed and several times later during the rest of this section.*] 'Z' thought the street that the house was in looked familiar, but couldn't place it. The fire killed about five people, and he thought the young man was the eldest or the second eldest of a group of brothers and sisters. 'Z' was picking up the name 'Graham', who he thought was the young man, and Graham was trying to get the family together so that they could move into the light. At that point 'Y' came in and said that one had found the light, but not the rest. 'Z' announced that Graham had gathered them together and that the nurse was also in attendance, as some healing was needed. Shortly they had all 'drifted' into the light.

A minute later the lights flashed but nobody had a link, however, the clicking of my pen (to record the light changes) disturbed 'Z'! Ninety seconds later the lights changed again and 'Y' at once said that she had this round table, around which were 'waifs and strays'. A big woman came in with a large pot of 'stew' for them, as they were all extremely hungry. The woman was looking after these children who had lost their parents from the bombing during the Second World War. 'Y' thought that all the children were under ten years old. 'Z' said that he had also linked in to this, and mentioned that he had Bluebell behind him. 'Y' then observed that three of the boys were brothers and that they were starved. 'Z' reported that Bluebell had apples for them! 'Y' next announced that they were 'floating' into the light and going to get healing. The others were wondering where the three brothers had gone and 'Y' told them about the lovely place where they could also go. Within a minute the whole lot, including the woman, were away into the light. [*During this last bit there was a loud noise on the digital recording, as if somebody had hit the table quite hard. But I have no recollection that an event such as that ever happened; this noise was also on the tape recording but due to the mild interference on the tape it was not very noticeable.*] A bit later 'Y' reported that they had all turned round and said, "What a wonderful world".

'Z' asked 'X' if she had got anything. Then 'Y' whispered about a star in the corner (to the light) – our 'Star of the East'? The lights went several times, and then 'X' asked if anybody else could hear the beeping sound that she was hearing, but nobody could. [*The interference on the tape recording increased substantially at this point, also the lights flickered several times. The interference only lasted a few minutes and then went clear again to the end of the tape.*] When asked, 'X' said it was like the engaged tone on the telephone.

Nothing happened for quite a while and then the tape finished with a loud click that made 'X' jump. At this point, when I was just about to close, I asked if anybody had anything. 'Y' commented that she was just about to speak. She had a woman with her whose name was 'Barbara' and that she had died of a brain haemorrhage, very suddenly, it felt like her head exploded. 'Y' reported that the nurse had come to Barbara – and that the nurse's name was 'Samantha'. 'Z' got a fit of sneezing at that point! Samantha was reassuring Barbara and shortly they went into the light.

We thanked all those who had come to help those people to go into the light and those who were helping us. Then we came back to normal awareness. There was a short discussion afterwards, and I reported that the picture had been 'going' again throughout the meeting. 'Z' closed the circle.

After this point the circle changed direction and later personnel. It eventually came to a close over three years later.

Personal Opinion

As you may have discerned from the previous reports, my experience of 'Rescue Work' was nil at the start of the Willow Circle. Subsequent involvement with Doris was limited, as indeed it was with the second closed circle also. However, enough happened to give me plenty of 'food for thought' and to form some understanding of what it was about. I know there are some circles that concentrate on this work full time and aid many who we might see as 'stuck', even those who might be difficult or awkward, or even some who could be classed as unpleasant, nasty or repulsive. Truly, I have great admiration for those that dedicate themselves to such work.

Other people dismiss 'Rescue Work' as a lot of nonsense, saying it is entirely unnecessary, that none need rescued and that God ensures that no soul gets 'lost'. Yet, it is spirit that initiates this work, not material humans. There is the phrase: 'God helps those who help themselves'. Once we come to an understanding that we are all one – then it is our duty to help all to get to the light, to raise 'ourselves' towards the higher realms of universal love, to get ever closer to God. God does not wave his/her magic wand – we (in the material and in spirit) are here to be of service, to do "God's work" at whatever level we may be at present. Love never turns it's back on those in need.

Willow Circle:

To start with, the Willow Circle taught me much about the basics. I well remember that after White Arrow had come through for the first time at my third meeting (15/12/94), Audrey declared that her experience was unusual – it was as if she had no stomach. This is not entirely unexpected when one considers that as one makes progress in spirit, so one becomes less 'earthy'. A higher spirit will have left behind such notions as eating, intestines and so forth! Chi later explained (15/02/96) that it was difficult to come back to the material world and, "not realise that you do not have to carry this burden of the material...it is a lesson that we have to learn when we become guides." At the circle before this 'John' was welcomed to our circle for the first time, and he came with his wheelchair. He had had a spastic condition when on earth, and consequently would have found himself excluded from much of 'normal' society, which is why he was so pleased that we accepted him. Rather than 'rescue', this was part of the process of normalising his mind and experience. To know that he was accepted by fellow human beings, so that he could be reintegrated in his mind and become a self-confident spirit. Mind is key when one passes to spirit – thought there becomes action. John had already taken his first steps on this road, when Chi told us on 22/02/96, that he was now going to school and thoroughly enjoyed his art lessons.

Something similar was involved with the cockney 'Joe', who had a very rough early life without parents, and relied on the kindness of prostitutes and artful theft to survive. This was in Victorian times. He eventually got a job as a lighterman, but got murdered. His best friend seemed to be his dog 'Jack'. Joe didn't have much of a chance in such a society, so he was intrigued by us, and finding a friendly reception wanted to come back. So rather than 'rescue', I think that it was more of a case of 'stabilization'. He also was getting taught in spirit, and enjoyed learning woodcarving and making boats.

The very first person that was brought to the Willow Circle had been a nursing nun from the Sacred Heart Order. While on a mercy mission in Gambia, her group was surrounded by guerillas and then killed – certainly a traumatic event. We were told that her emotions were still earthbound and that she had not got over her death. By thinking of her while we were engaged in Spiritual Healing, she was connected to healing work again. I think what she needed was a chance to calm down and be at peace with like minds. She needed to 'touch' the earth plane again and 're-balance'. Near the end of the Willow Circle we were told that she was doing well and was happy, helping the children and seeing to the sick.

A totally different character was our 'X' or Mr. 'Hallelujah' (20/07/95). This lay preacher was just continuing his earthly mission! I dare say he was taken to many circles until, as Chi told us, he will gradually calm down, and then find a new work in spirit. Some people just need the time and space to really adjust to their new environment.

The only other 'rescue' involved the sad case of young Gladys. On the verge of giving birth, this seventeen year old took some drugs – probably a cry for help really. However, it was just a bit too much for her heart and she and her baby died. When she realised the result of her actions, she was distraught – not for herself, but for her baby who could not now experience her life on Earth. So Gladys and her baby Geraldine were welcomed to our circle. Chi told us that she was still in a state of shock and had to be given time, and that this is why she needed this connection. Once we knew that she liked 'Little Red Rooster' by The Rolling Stones, we played it at the start of the circle every time. Apparently she used to dance to this, flapping her arms like a chicken. So a bit later, when she had been assigned a job of taking care of the little ones, she did this dance to make them laugh. At that stage Gladys was well on the way to recovery, although she would need to have a bit of resilience to let Geraldine reincarnate a bit later.

The circle didn't really do any 'rescue'. What spirit did was to use us – knowing that we would be willing participants. First, to calm the problem spirit down, taking them to a safe, peaceful place and reassuring them that they were with friends. This gave that particular spirit the opportunity to stabilise, find their bearings again, and then to move on. If the Willow Circle had continued, I'm quite sure that this work would have not just continued, but perhaps have tried to deal with more difficult cases. Chi (7/09/95) did say that they did wish to use us in rescue. However, I always presumed that meant that the present work that we were involved with was of a minor level. Unfortunately, the Willow Circle closed when Bernard moved and we never got to experience any deeper work. I also regretted that we never got to hear some of the higher philosophy. It would have been fascinating to hear what Khahoom could have told us!

The only other incident that was referred to as 'rescue' occurred on 18/05/95. It seemed to quite clearly allude to helping J.F. Kennedy, and that it was only partly successful. Why he should still be in such a state is a question that immediately springs to mind, but if he didn't die immediately, then the trauma might be so great that he can't release that from his mind. I can only report what happened, and leave it to others to speculate further.

Meetings with Doris:

The first experience here was with 'Hugo' (12/09/99), the man who wasn't very friendly at the start. The reason for this soon became apparent as parts of his life were revealed when he was questioned. He had a condition in his left leg that went untreated and became gangrenous. Without medical help it spread and eventually killed him. Those around him were repelled by his condition and possibly feared that they would be infected, so he was shunned and isolated. This built up great resentment in his mind and distrust of others.

I would class this case as a 'rescue', maybe a 'soft' one, but still a rescue. He had thought he was in blackness and alone, his mental condition ensured that. However, seeing the light and the 'feelings that are here', he realised that he needed help and was willing to take it. Because he had been used to the dark, spirit only displayed a light outline around themselves, and treated him slowly and carefully, as they knew he would be apprehensive. The emotion in 'his' voice was evident, "no one held out their hand to me" and, "I can't believe that people want to help me". It was very satisfying when he finally went to the light.

'Arbuthnot' was easier to deal with. He stole a sheep – to feed his family – but was sentenced and hung. He had been listening to the previous encounter with Hugo, so had begun to realise that he didn't have to stay as he was. He had been told he was wicked to do such a thing, but he probably blamed himself more for leaving his children without somebody to look after them. Very quickly, he ran to the light.

At the next meeting (10/10/99) I was put to the test, and Doris couldn't help me, as she was the medium. This was one that failed to be rescued, and it preyed on my mind for a long time afterwards. Eric Foster died in great fear. His shipmate John Diamond may have been a Spiritualist, he knew that he would go to the light on death and had obviously aired his views to those around him. So near the end he told Eric to just hold onto him and the two of them would go together. However, this did not happen. Eric had only the thought of finding John; he wasn't interested in anything else. My first job should have been to calm him down, but this I failed to do. Let us hope another circle managed to get him over.

It was yet another example of the power of the mind, and why it is crucial that people understand that life does not end at what we call 'death'. The next phase of life is a 'mental environment' and how we think is very important. This was clearly shown in the very next two 'rescues'. First a woman died after a long illness, and just felt she had to stay where she was as that idea had been implanted in her mind during her life, maybe waiting for the 'last trump'. Her guide had been waiting for her to wake up, noting that her mind had been closed to the reality of spirit. With the help of some flowers – the first thing that she'd seen – she awoke, and eventually realised what a waste of time her 'sleeping' had been. Her guide then took her to the light. The second woman died in childbirth, and although her daughter survived, it would seem it was not too long before her child also died. Her daughter came to see her, but that didn't affect her thinking, expected nothing, as 'she had been naughty'. However, she did go to the light, and a man in an air force uniform came to thank us, as well revealing that he was at fault in this case.

It was shortly after this that Doris was told by spirit that it was 'attempted rescue', and that it was better described as 'helping lost souls'. Perhaps it was more like somebody in a strange city, and they have just lost their orientation, having unknowingly taken a left turn instead of just going straight ahead. However, some people have been indoctrinated to expect nothing, or to be in limbo, or that they are too sinful to be 'saved'. If they believe this, then they can indeed end up in darkness – until they can be redirected to the light.

At the next meeting (7/11/99) the first to come through was a spirit who didn't need a 'rescue', but still had regrets. She died by fire at about three years of age, just before Christmas, so never got to open her presents. She had been in spirit for around twelve years, but had missed the excitement of presents not only at Christmas but her birthdays as well. It was a reminder of how emotional needs can remain with a spirit for some time.

What proved to be the last 'rescue' sitting was next. A woman, who had died in the eighteenth century, but was now just waiting – waiting for someone. Once realisation came to her, she went to the light very quickly. This was another lesson for us. In the spirit world there is no conception of time, they do not have any need for clocks or watches, they are only of use in the material world.

Closed Circle:

This was a bit more disorganised than the previous two groups. Despite protocols being agreed and apparently accepted, some seemed to forget them. However, the start of the 'rescue work' (29/11/07) didn't really involve us at all, as a group of children and a few adults made their way to the light. The next, involving a young man called Eric, was interesting, in that he seemed to be 'held back' by his mother's thoughts. It did not take very long before he also went into the light. Yet again, the power of thought is shown. It shows that spirit are aware of our thoughts on the material plane.

On the next circle (6/12/07) a little old lady called Hilda was paralysed with fear of her 'master' in her earthly life. It took a bit of reassurance before she could move through to the light. Once fear has taken hold of someone, it is like they are frozen, transfixed in a state that could potentially take many earthly years to surmount.

After this, we had a bit of a muddle around two 'rescues'. One called Charles, had apparently died, but just carried on with his 'life', not realizing – or ignoring – that he didn't fit in with the material world. I suspect that these people understand that something is not quite right, but not knowing what to do, they ignore it and try to carry on as they usually did. His wife, having already died before him, came back in her earthly condition – in a wheelchair, and she and their Yorkshire terrier got him into the light.

Meanwhile, 'X' had a rough, drunk, cantankerous fellow to deal with, and was a bit frightened by it. Despite that, the man started praying, and that change in his thinking enabled spirit to nip in and take him into the light. It was a bit of a learning experience for 'X', that would be repeated. Those in circle should never let emotions or fear enter their work; otherwise the whole process can be negated.

The final one of that session was another case of where fear was a factor. A man was out fishing in the middle of a river. He was rooted to the spot, not daring to move. With plenty of reassurance, he slowly turned and made his way to the riverbank where a friend was waiting, and then they went to the light. This person must have died, drowned when the water overwhelmed him. Yet, that horrifying fear just before he died stayed with him after the event, rooting him in that moment. He certainly could have been described as 'stuck'.

At the next meeting (13/12/07) we had a coalman, Mr. Archer, who was trying to do his normal work despite dying due to a serious accident. He didn't want to remember the accident due to the pain associated with it. It was dealt with by spirit, who sent in a nurse to take him to the light.

Meanwhile 'X' had someone who was in despair, sitting in a bleak landscape, often the sort of place where people find themselves if they have lost hope. After much reassurance we managed to turn him towards his mother and family, who brought him into the light. I was particularly interested in what 'X' had to say at the beginning, that she saw a person in a long blue gown with his hands clasped in front of him – observing / standing guard. I assume he was the young teenager's 'Guardian' or the spirit who brought him to us.

Soon 'X' was in another testing contact, where she felt herself 'become the woman', which of course was an excessive emotional condition that she should have resisted. Anyhow, it concerned a woman in an old peoples' home, with mobility and other issues, who died. She clung onto her material life, probably not knowing what else to do, but hoping that husband, Bertie, would come and sort things out. He did come, and he did take her into the light. Bertie was a vicar in the material life, and interestingly said that he now realises that there is more to it.

Two people came through at the start of the next circle (20/12/07), a woman to 'X' and a man to 'Z', both had committed suicide. The woman had been under great stress and money problems, and now was apprehensive due to what she had done. With reassurance, she calmed down and went to the light. The man had been due to get married and his 'bride' let him down very badly. Under this emotional turmoil, he took his own life. However, 'Z' gave him reassurance, and he went into the light.

Shortly after this 'Z' had a man called George, who was into motorbikes and a bit of a daredevil. It was this that ended his material life, and had been in limbo now for about twenty-eight years. Although he had never 'believed in any of this', seeing some of his mates waiting, he went quickly into the light. It was the lack of belief that kept him mentally limited to limbo.

'X' next had a hard man, a docker, who had made his wife's life miserable. Now on his own, he finally realised his mistakes and was 'crying like a baby in repentance'. This change of mind was the key, and soon his young daughter clasped his hand and took him into the light.

The final one was a little boy of about nine years of age, called Martin. He wanted to see his friends, and thought 'X' was trying to get him in to put him to bed. Bluebell solved the problem by taking him through to the light.

In the New Year, (10/01/08) we started with 'X' having a young teenage boy, Peter, who seemed to have died when he fell down a well or shaft. With reassurance and encouragement, Peter soon rose up the shaft and reunited with his dog went into the light. Animals can be very helpful in these situations. However, the next one was a little confusing as it involved a goat that represented a person, Billy, who had a rift with his brother Joe. Joe had come to make peace with Billy, and with the mother also there, both went to the light.

The last was connected to another emotional trauma, a lady who was playing the organ, had been badly let down and not got over it. She wanted to see her mother, but **not** 'him'. She loved playing and singing, and adored horses. Again, with a bit of reassurance, she went to the light and was reunited with her mother.

The first 'rescue' at the next circle (17/01/08) was the longest that we ever had, taking at least twenty-five minutes before he went to the light. It would seem that a young Polish man had an accident in his car, possibly due to black ice, and died immediately, his spirit ejected out of the material body. He was confused and didn't understand what we were saying, or what was happening to him. Thankfully, spirit sent in a doctor and a nurse to calm him down, and a spirit who spoke Polish explained the situation and took him to the light. If one has not thought about death on the material plane, then to find oneself suddenly in that situation would be utterly bewildering.

'X' had a tearful young boy of about seven years old who wanted his twin brother Billy. The family appeared, and that was all that was needed, as Bobby ran to them in the light. However, during the first 'rescue', 'X' had somebody else. On being asked about it, she described a macabre scene: a naked young lad with long hair being pulled from what looked like white sand, but his hands were bound. It was good to hear that he finally rose into the light.

The next one was also disturbing, as it involved a very young teenage girl, Clare, who had been abused by her father or stepfather. A 'neutral' person, we think a nurse, was the one who came and took her into the light.

The final 'rescue' was with 'Y'. She was an old grandmother, who had come to stand by a very little girl until she died. Then the two of them went into the light. I think this was mainly for our education. Spirit knew this child would die, and who better to take her into spirit than her grandmother.

A soldier was the first at our next circle (24/01/08), who responded to orders from spirit, and marched off into the light. Then it was Joe, a farmer, who had hanged himself. Like many other suicides, he was a bit apprehensive of how others of his family would react to him, as he knew it was wrong to do such a thing. With encouragement and reassurance, he went to the light.

Then it was another case where fear was prominent. At a circus, an animal had mauled a man and he was terror-struck, frozen to the spot. A doctor and nurse from spirit helped him by giving him 'an injection' to sedate him, and then carried him to the light. Of course, it wasn't a 'real' injection; the action would change the mind of the recipient, which was all that was needed.

Shortly after that there was a man who died due to his heart, but had other medical problems as well. This person had never really thought about death or the afterlife, despite his health issues, consequently he was still sitting in a chair at his home. He saw the light, but was apprehensive. A nurse came and took him by the hand and led him into the light. Yes, it really is that easy.

The first link (31/01/08) at the next session was with a man called Bernard, who somewhat confused, was looking for his wife. In the material life he had Alzheimer's disease, but didn't have it now. He quickly saw the light and went in to meet his wife. This is an interesting case. Dementia in its many forms – including Alzheimer's – is often a progressive deterioration of the brain, affecting memory, emotions, behavioural issues and even language. The mind therefore has problems connecting with the body, but at death it is then free and the person is back to 'normal'. So Bernard suddenly was 'free' and naturally wanted to know where his wife was, as his memory had been impaired at that particular stage in his life when she died. So naturally at first he was confused.

The next one was slightly hilarious. An elderly and stout lady died falling down the stairs into a cellar while on her way to fetch some coal. A spirit team, with ropes, arranged to haul her out of it, before they got her over to the light. Presumably, she still thought herself to be alive and so of a certain condition and weight!

Following this was a man who died with a heart attack. He was a bit annoyed as he still had some things he wanted to do, but with reassurance he passed quickly into the light. Quickly 'Y' linked in with potholers, one man and two women who got caught by rising water. They followed a spirit person to the surface and then were taken into the light.

The last person was another suicide, a young man who hung himself, though he said, "I didn't mean to do it". Perhaps it was something like Gladys' case from the Willow Circle, like a cry for help that went a little too far. The doctor and nurse from spirit attended him and took him to the light.

It was significant that at the subsequent circle, I executed an exercise that Doris had taught me, to call everyone back to normal awareness promptly.

When we opened out after that 'Z' saw a man who asked him if there was a chance of us helping on the astral plane, where there were hardened souls, tramps and ragamuffins. I didn't see this as coincidence. I was sure that spirit would ask us to do harder work, and had been thinking of doing that exercise for a while. Spirit could read my mind and so responded immediately. 'Z' said that he would have to discuss it with the group first.

'Z' then reported that three lads had drowned, but they quickly saw the light and went over. 'Y' mentioned that she had seen a 'Joe' in a wheelchair, as he had part of one leg removed, but that he had disappeared. However, a few minutes later she saw Joe, and told us that he had gone to bring back some of his mates. Soon she said that they were marching into the light.

'Z' reported that he had a climber, still climbing mountains, as he had not come to terms with having died. Somebody from spirit came and led the climber into the light. Yet again, here is an example of someone trying to carry on a 'normal' life after they had died.

Next 'Z' said he had a 'George', a Christian – though not a very good one – who was looking for his mother Isobel. Very quickly he went to the light and met his mother, who told 'Z' that George hadn't been bad at all, *that it was just his way of thinking*. Shortly after that 'Z' announced that he had a 'Duncan' who had died in a car crash. He made his way to the light and was greeted by his granddad.

A difficult challenge was presented about five minutes later. There was a young man in a house who had hanged himself over his girlfriend and other things. He was stuck and couldn't move on, with a lot of anger in him as well as the anguish, and his mind kept going back to the house. 'Z' was trying to pacify him, and despite both doctor and nurse from spirit attending him, he was very stubborn. It is difficult for some of these emotional suicides; they have a range of emotions and thoughts, often changing from being distraught to great anger. Then the man's dog came in and his attitude started to change, and soon all went to the light together.

Two weeks later (6/03/08) things went fairly smoothly. First 'Z' reported that he had a young man, 'Joe', who had died when his motorbike hit a lorry on a bend. 'Y' then said that she had a 'Mary Ellen' who was looking for Joe, and soon both went over to the light. Next 'Z' had a miner, who had died in a cave-in, but the miner was reliving the pain he had felt, and 'Z' was picking up the symptoms. However, this was overcome and

'Z' managed to get the miner and about nine of his workmates to go to the light. Quite often a medium will pick up physical symptoms from a spirit, especially one who is thinking about the way he or she died. It can be unpleasant but nothing more than that. This can be useful in mental mediumship, to be able to give how a loved one died and from what condition. Once that is done, the medium will ask for the condition to be taken away.

'Z' saw a little girl holding her mother's hand, they were looking for the little girl's brother, who been left in a hospital. The mother and daughter had died before the brother, so he was a bit 'stuck'. A nurse from spirit helped and the little girl gave him his teddy, so they all happily went into the light together.

At the next circle (13/03/08) 'Z' got another young man who had committed suicide. He hung himself, but was now full of remorse at what he had done. His grandmother came and led him to the light. Not only are grandparents very useful in the material life, but often also when in spirit.

After this, a woman had not got over losing her children in a house fire, caused by a chip pan. She blamed herself and was in mental anguish. However, seeing her children at the doorway to the light, she went through very quickly. Her mind was forever going over the chip pan and fire, and consequently she was rooted in the material. But seeing her children waiting for her changed all that.

'Z' thought that the next one went back to the Second World War. A plane had come down in fog and all were killed. An RAF captain was trying to persuade his crew to go to the light. The nurse from spirit went to help and soon all were over. It is not entirely clear, but it is possible that the captain had passed over, and now was going back to get the crew to move on.

A week later (20/03/08) the first contact was with a 'Lenny' who had lots of health problems in life, but despite this hadn't thought much about death and what came next. His wife Edna was waiting for him, on the occasion of their wedding anniversary, and he soon went with her into the light.

The next one involved a thirteen-year-old boy who received a head injury while riding his bicycle. However, 'Brian' was concerned that his siblings would see his disfigurement due to the injury. When asked whom he would like to see, it was his great uncle, who duly obliged. What I liked about this case was that going into the light he also took his bag and bicycle with him!

The following one involved another house fire. This time about five people were killed. One had found the light, but one of the eldest was trying to get the others together to follow. After the nurse from spirit attended, they all passed into the light.

Then we were back to the Second World War, with a woman who seemed to be looking after lots of orphans from the bombing. She was trying to feed these children – all less than ten years old – as best she could, but they were all hungry. Three brothers were starving and Bluebell came without us asking for her, giving them some lovely apples and taking them into the light. The rest were wondering where the brothers had gone, and 'Y' supplied the answer and got them all, including the woman, into the light.

The last case was a 'Barbara', who died of a very sudden brain haemorrhage. Apparently it had felt like her head exploded. 'Y' reported that the spirit nurse had come in, and that the nurse was called Samantha. She reassured Barbara and then took her into the light. I can understand how such an experience could confuse and disorientate a person, and indeed could be quite frightening. There may be some similarities here with the JFK situation.

There is an interesting aspect to how these situations were handled by the various mediums. In the Willow Circle the medium allowed the different helpers/teachers/guides to speak through her in their own voices. This also applied to others, like 'Joe' and the lay preacher.

In the meetings with Doris it was mixed. Mostly it was the medium reporting on the person that they had with them, but on the odd occasion they would convey direct speech, though with the mediums own voice. Doris herself let the potential spirit to be rescued speak through her ('Eric Foster' 10/10/99). She sometimes asked the mediums to let the spirit speak through them, though they used the voice of the medium.

As far as I can recollect, not once did a spirit connected to a rescue situation speak through a medium in the closed circle. The mediums just related what the spirit that was with them was saying, feeling or doing.

Before moving on to my conclusions, it would be negligent of me not to mention more about that plane, sphere, realm or level, that we find ourselves in after 'death' or 'passing over' – the astral world.

The Astral World

There are some who like to divide the astral world into two levels: the upper or higher astral and the lower astral. However, rather than a definite line or barrier between each (involving many levels) there is rather a gradual merging of one into another, so that no sudden or dramatic change is necessary. Indeed the astral interpenetrates our material world, which often makes the transition at 'death' very easy and comfortable. Like all planes of spirit, it is a realm of consciousness; it is where the mind has greater importance.

On Earth we can think evil thoughts towards somebody, yet deceive them with smiles upon our faces. Not so in the astral plane. Your thoughts can be perceived and read by all around you. It is your mental attitude that will determine where, or at what level, you will reside. Whether you can be with like-minded people in the light-filled areas, or in the darker areas, or even without any companions at all. At the lowest astral level are found those who have not been able to restrain their fanaticism, obsessions, lasciviousness and fury. This becomes a real self-made hell for them, as, without a material body, they cannot satisfy their desires and passions. Yet, ultimately, in time they can start to control their thoughts and be able to make progress to higher levels. All are given the opportunity to progress further, by changing their outlook and/or helping others in many different ways. There is no preference given to social class, position, religion, colour or country, all are treated as equals. Though the 'heavens' or 'hells' that are experienced are due to what those people made for themselves by their lives on Earth.

That is why spirit take so much time, and trouble to themselves, in order to try to get us at a better level of understanding and more ready for the astral world. For all on earth will have to travel there, some for a shorter time before moving on to the higher spiritual spheres, but many for long ages before they have mastered their thoughts and emotions.

Spirit tell us that looking down upon the Earth they see it covered by huge grey clouds, some areas very dark and only the occasional spot of light visible. That is the spiritual state of the world and the astral plane near it. No wonder spirit work so tirelessly to get through and urge all who will listen to change their thinking. To try to get us to be more loving and helpful to others, to create harmony between people and to think less materially, less about ourselves and more about being of service to humanity in general. It is what we **do** and **think** in this world that will determine our place in the astral one.

Here on Earth we are building our foundations of our future. Learning from experience what is best and what is worst, what is the right way to live and what is the wrong way, what is good and what is evil. This Earth life may be one small step on our journey into eternity, but it is important that it is taken in the right direction.

For many it will be a natural transition into a commonplace environment, with recognised friends and family. Familiar due to having visited it during their sleep state, when the astral body has travelled there. The astral body is a finer duplicate of the material one, and it is the silver cord (or astral cord) that connects the two. During the sleep state, when the physical body and everyday mental activity is less active, the astral body can visit and communicate with the 'dead' (and other astral bodies of those still living in the material world). Thus there is a sense of continuity and indeed familiarity when we do 'die' or 'pass over'.

All living things have an astral body, including animals. This was demonstrated to a friend, who had looked after two dogs that belonged to his neighbours while they had a holiday for about seven days. He made the mistake of letting the dogs sleep on his bed. Once his neighbours returned, he was disturbed nearly every night by the dogs visiting his bedroom in their astral bodies. He could feel their weight and presence on his bed and distinctly heard the thud on the carpet when one jumped off the bed. After about five days of this he awoke in the morning at around 4.20am, and saw the head of one dog looking at him. Telling them to go away had little effect, until he changed his response and just told them to lie down quietly. This had the desired affect.

Not long afterwards, he again looked after the dogs, this time for two weeks. When the neighbours returned, he once more experienced the presence of the dogs at night. He reported that he clearly saw one dog at close quarters and had noticed that it didn't breathe! I explained that as it was the astral bodies of the dogs, they wouldn't – the breathing would be occurring in the material bodies of the dogs next door. The material bodies would be on 'automatic pilot' mode, with the heart still beating and pumping blood around the system, and the lungs taking in oxygen etc.

An interesting point here is that the astral body does not have awareness of pain. That is why those who sometimes have an 'out-of-body' experience during surgery, always report being free of any pain and find the feeling so wonderful, and are often very reluctant to return to their material body.

The astral plane is only the very first step, so there will be no 'heaven' where we laze around listening to beautiful music with our feet up all day. We will have much work to do to in order to attain the higher levels in the astral, before starting the journey to spiritual spheres. We should know by now that nothing is gained without effort and even suffering, so it is in the astral. We have to purify ourselves of all the dross of the material before we can be at the proper state to progress further.

Conclusions

First let us deal with the semantics. The word rescue conjures up an idea of something dramatic, like a lifeboat saving the crew of a ship sinking in a storm. However, a rescue doesn't necessarily have to be a drama at all. So the word can involve a wide range of meaning depending on the content and context. You can *love* your God, *love* your partner, and also *love* ice cream. We don't have to invent a large range of new words to understand *love* in each of those phrases.

At the time of writing this, we in the UK are waiting for Article 50 to be triggered so that we can leave the European Union. 'Brexit means Brexit', but it seems that there is also a 'hard' Brexit and a 'soft' Brexit. I dare say we could have a hard rescue, medium rescue, soft rescue and featherweight rescue! While assembling this book I have become more neutral about its use than previously. The word has been around long enough for most people to know what it refers to, and so I see little point in trying to invent another.

The reason that rescue work is needed, is because some people after their death have not progressed to the next level. They find themselves in earthly-like situations, or in lonely landscapes or darkness. This is due to how they think. The main barriers are fear, anger and hate. Fear is very debilitating, rooting them in that emotion and in the material, so they are unable to move on. Anger and hate do the same thing, until they can change that emotion and change their thinking.

There are a huge number of different ways and situations in human death. Some die and not really know that they have done so! Others in this situation may find that things are not quite normal, but just carry on, as that is all that they can think to do. You will have read about this in the previous text, as also suicides, those who died in accidents, in war, or illness, and those who have thought they would be in limbo, or have to wait until they 'awakened'. What all need is a change in their thoughts. It is for this reason that rescue work is needed.

When a normal circle forms, there is a harmony created, an energy that can be seen by those in spirit as light. This light may attract those who need rescue, or spirit may guide them to it. As a rescue is taking place, those others that are there will be able to see what is going on and learn from it, and may pass over into the spirit world without any contact with the circle. Some could be in trauma due to a sudden accident, so may need calming down and to be stabilized. Most need reassurance, and some need love, or a human contact to 're-orientate', to be in harmony again. For others it may just be a case of 'finding their bearings' and regaining their 'balance'. For all it is to sort out their thinking, and if this is done it is an easy step to move into spirit and carry on with their new life.

It is to be regretted that more people do not think about their death and what may come after it. Even people who have serious medical conditions may never do so. This may be due to fear, fear of the unknown. Much of this rescue work would be unnecessary if it was understood that life continues in the spirit world.

However, there are in addition those who consciously choose to stay where they are. People who have such a close attachment to a home, to particular material possessions, etc., may fiercely decide that they will not leave. As it says in the Bible: "For where your treasure is, there will your heart be also" (Mat 6.21 and Luke 12.34). There are those who have a belief in Heaven or Hell, and that they will be taken to one or the other. If they have not been good attenders at their church, or may have committed some 'sins', they may speculate that it could be probable that Hell might be the likely destination. In this scenario they make the decision to stay where they are, no matter what inconveniences that it may throw up. It is hoped that in time they may change their thinking, or connect with a material medium who can assist them, or that spirit will at the appropriate time step in so they may be able to go forward and progress. We have free will, and this is respected by the spirit world.

All this just reinforces the truth that mind is the key factor. Mind is that eternal part of us that comes into its own after death of the physical body.

For the realms of spirit are realms of consciousness. Planet Earth – and no doubt many others throughout the universe – is merely a school where we are given the chance to learn the basic ideas of spirituality. Where we can make our blunders, but are given the chance to pick ourselves up and do better next time. Where we are tested, but yet guided and encouraged by our true friends and teachers in spirit. When we eventually reach the appropriate stage in our spiritual evolution, we can then continue outwith the material environment, going onward through the spiritual spheres or planes.

Before ending this book, it would be remiss of me not to include two other situations where a rescue circle can be helpful, not just to the 'dead' but also to those living in the material. This is where there is an 'attachment' or where 'possession' is involved. Attachments are usually found where a recently deceased person's spirit becomes linked to the aura of a living human being. Often this can be dealt with quite easily and quickly if one is aware of it. I wrote about my personal experience of this in my first book, "An Ordinary Life…?". However, if not dealt with, in time it can have an adverse affect on the health of the material person.

Possession can be a bit harder to treat, due to the intent and negative energy of the particular spirit. As an example, let us think of an alcoholic, who is hooked on alcohol as others are on drugs, and that he then dies, but his mind is so fixed on drink that he does not pass over properly to spirit. He may stay around a particular pub, and when he sees somebody with a tendency to drink, may try to influence that person to become like he was. There are lots of other scenarios that can be involved. This requires a strong rescue circle to free the living person from the 'dead'.

However, for most people who lead ordinary lives and who try to do their best, 'dying' or passing over into the light of spirit is a simple and easy affair. Most do so without any problems at all. Nevertheless, there is a vast array of humankind and an equally vast variety of attitudes, thoughts and characters. It is nice to know that there are rescue circles that can help those who find themselves in unexpected difficulties.

There are very few books that are devoted to rescue work. I hope that this small contribution can be of some help to those who may not have come across it themselves. Hopefully it can throw some light on the subject, and be a starting point for their further investigation.